THE TRIUMPH OF THE WATER WITCH

IOANA IERONIM

THE Triumph OF THE Water Witch

translated by ADAM J SORKIN

with IOANA IERONIM

BLOODAXE BOOKS

Copyright © Ioana Ieronim 1992, 2000
Translation copyright © Adam J. Sorkin & Ioana Ieronim 2000

ISBN: 1 85224 483 6

First published 2000 by
Bloodaxe Books Ltd,
P.O. Box 1SN,
Newcastle upon Tyne NE99 1SN.

Bloodaxe Books Ltd acknowledges
the financial assistance of Northern Arts.

Thanks are due to the Arts Council of England
for providing a translation grant for this book.

Cover printing by J. Thomson Colour Printers Ltd, Glasgow.

Printed in Great Britain by
Cromwell Press Ltd, Trowbridge, Wiltshire.

ACKNOWLEDGEMENTS

Acknowledgements are due to the editors and publishers of the following publications in which a number of these poems first appeared, sometimes in slightly different versions: *Antietam Review*: 'Journey', 'Annular Eclipse', 'At the Beginning', 'The Fates', 'The Triumph of the Water Witch', 'Parents and Child', 'When I Departed'; *The Blue Penny Quarterly*: 'The Crown', 'Master of the Mountains', 'Orphans from Tradition', 'Arranging the Wardrobe', 'Mother's Crying', 'The Priest', 'Black Bread', 'The Brick Kiln'; *The Chattahoochee Review*: 'At the Bus Stop, in Winter'; *Connecticut Review*: 'Words', 'The Ball', 'The Man', 'Landscape', 'At Home' (along with an earlier version of a section of the Translator's Introduction); *The Dexter Review*: 'My Friends' House', 'I Know How to Speak'; *The Fiddlehead*: 'In the Street Outside the Grocery'; *The Ohio Poetry Review*: 'The Chest with Old Things', 'At the Pharmacy', 'Neighbours', 'Airy Structures'; *Oxford Magazine*: 'At the Bend of the Don', 'At the Old Fortress', 'Summer Afternoon', 'Your Life Will Be Like This'; *Quarter After Eight*: 'In Need', 'Ida', 'The Deaf Man', 'Easter', 'Rosi', 'The Metamorphosis'; *Rio*: 'The Bârsa Land' ['At sunset parting the stalks of wheat like a wave...'], 'The Measure of Time', 'Works and Days'; *Visions International*: 'Emigration', 'Partisans'.

Adam J. Sorkin is grateful to Penn State University for support of some of his work on these translations. Warm thanks to two Penn State colleagues, poet Robin Becker and fiction writer Peter Schneeman, and to a third friend, poet and translator Carolyne Wright, all of whom read over this manuscript in its final stages and gave judicious and helpful counsel. And not least of all, if last, thanks to Nancy, for careful reading, for honest reactions, for good suggestions, for everything.

CONTENTS

9   *Translator's Introduction*
16   *Note on the pronunciation of Romanian letters*

18   Journey
18   Annular Eclipse
19   At the Beginning
20   That Winter
22   The Fates
23   The Bârsa Land
24   The Triumph of the Water Witch
25   Parents and Child
26   Partisans
27   Your Life Will Be Like This
28   At the Pharmacy
29   Christmas
30   Ida
32   Epiphany
33   The Crown
34   Walls and Life
35   Master of the Mountains
36   Friends in Need
38   The Measure of Time
38   My Friends' House
40   Neighbours
41   Misch
42   The Deaf Man
43   An Orphan from Tradition
44   The Century Was Breaking in Half
45   Works and Days
47   Arranging the Wardrobe
48   Another Season
49   Mother's Crying
50   Sunday Morning
50   The Ball
52   Aunt Edith and Uncle Fritz
55   Words
56   Holidays
57   Easter
58   At the Bus Stop, in Winter

59 Evening
60 Ţica Doaii
61 On the Dobrice
63 At the Bend of the Don
63 Rosi
64 Refugees
65 The Chest with Old Things
65 On the Way to School
67 The Doctor
70 The Metamorphosis
71 Summer Afternoon
72 Landscape
73 The Priest
74 The Brick Kiln
75 Black Bread
76 Discipline
77 In the Street Outside the Grocery
77 Airy Structures
78 Healing
80 At the Old Fortress
81 The First Warning
82 The Bârsa Land
83 At Home
83 I Know How to Speak
84 The Man
86 Emigration
87 When I Departed

88 *Notes*
95 *Biographical notes*

TRANSLATOR'S INTRODUCTION

The contemporary Romanian poet Ioana Ieronim – also my co-translator – is the author of seven volumes of poetry as well as numerous articles, reviews, and translations from English, French, German and Swedish. The 63 poems gathered here comprise roughly two-thirds of Ieronim's most recent book, *The Triumph of the Water Witch* (in Romanian, *Triumful paparudei*), published in Bucharest in 1992. The selection is by the poet, who has made small changes and additions to her texts in the process of our cooperating on this translation, and the order of the poems remains the same as in the original.

Ieronim is one of the most important and highly respected members of the generation of her country's writers who began to publish their books in the 1970s, a generation in which women were particularly prominent. Authors such as Ana Blandiana (who emerged earlier, in the previous decade), Ileana Mălăncioiu, Daniela Crăsnaru, prose writer Gabriela Adameşteanu, and, later, Mariana Marin became known internationally, along with Liliana Ursu, Denisa Comănescu and Grete Tartler, for their outstanding literary merit among the many compelling voices of Romania's poetry-rich culture. As a group, but most particularly the five listed first, they also became emblematic of the opposition for their increasingly outspoken resistance to the worsening repression and deprivation of Nicolae Ceauşescu's communist dictatorship.

Ioana Ieronim was born on 9 January 1947 in the Transylvanian Saxon community of Râşnov, a town on the Bârsa River not far from Dracula's reconstructed castle at Bran and near the city of Braşov in the arc of the Carpathians. In a once typical East European fashion, Râşnov was composed of more or less separate, but not exclusive, sections: an area largely made up of ethnic Germans, or Saxons (they called the town Rosenau); the Romanian village, as everyone termed it; and a gypsy quarter in addition. Her own background is Romanian, although her family was one of the few Romanian families living in the Saxon district. Ieronim had a German childhood education and then went to high school and higher studies in Bucharest, graduating in 1970 from the University of Bucharest with a degree in English language and literature. Her first book of poetry, *Early Spring*, came out in 1979, and she published five other collections during the following decade: *Mythological Project* (1981), *The Curtain* (1983), *Eclogue* (1984), *Poems* (1986) and *Monday Morning* (1987).

9

The writer's pen name – Ieronim is the Romanian version of Hieronymus – is a pseudonym that she borrowed from the Dutch painter Bosch in 1971 and has kept ever since. At the time, a magazine publisher decided that her family name, Moroiu, which can mean 'spirit' or 'ghost', was inappropriate, probably in absurd accordance with the dictates of dialectical materialism.

While pursuing her career as a poet, Ieronim worked for 15 years as an editor at the Scientific and Encyclopaedic Publishing House in Bucharest, and then, after the December 1989 revolution, at the much esteemed occasional journal of international culture, *The Twentieth Century*. In 1992, she accepted appointment as a diplomat, serving as Cultural Counsellor in the Romanian Embassy in Washington, D.C., until the summer of 1996. Since then she has worked as coordinator of public affairs for the Soros Foundation in Bucharest and as an editor at *22*, the leading political, social and cultural weekly of Romanian intellectuals supporting democratic change, which takes its name from the date, December 22, when the Ceauşescu government fell. Ieronim started her present position as a Program Director for the Fulbright Commission in Romania in the summer of 1998.

During this period of intense involvement in foreign affairs and non-governmental organisations, she has continued to write, especially in the latter half of the 1990s, and she is involved now in a number of concurrent book projects: a selected poems including recent works not previously gathered between the covers of a book, an illustrated volume of impressions of Bucharest at the beginning of the new millennium, a translation of the poems of American writer John Balaban, and a book of dialogues with the eminent Romanian-born pianist Lory Wallfisch.

The Triumph of the Water Witch takes form almost exclusively in poems of very long lines like verse paragraphs whose style can at times seem situated between prose and poetry, transparency and mediation. There is a loose narrative link among all the poems (there are 92 in the original). In their most immediate subject-matter, the sequence of works depicts the coming of Soviet-style communism to a village in 'the deepest extremity' of Europe and its impact on the central character and observer's girlhood: 'the movement of the world balanced on the shoulders of a child'. I can remember Ieronim describing the volume to me during an unofficial, private conversation in her Bucharest flat when I first came to know her in early August 1989, a particularly tense time when the walls and governments of communist political practice were wobbling or collapsing all around Romania's borders. This was some five months before the overthrow of the Ceauşescu government, and our meeting, without proper authorisation, was not without a degree of risk for her. Ieronim was then in the throes of writing these poems in the increasingly bleak political climate and restrictive censorship of Romania in the late 1980s. Confessing a feeling of fatalism and, in the same breath, demonstrating open-eyed practicality, she told me that she was sure she would never see the manuscript in print. Nonetheless, she made it explicit that she felt compelled to compose this collection out of a deep moral need to bear witness to, and simultaneously dissent from, Romania's totalitarian régime – not just its despotism, brutality and corruption but also, with an even greater sense of horror, the corollary degradation of human dignity, individuality and integrity.

While Ieronim was growing up, first as a young child under the postwar Soviet occupation, then as an older teenager under home-grown communist rule, 'the century was breaking in half', a phrase that she re-echoes in her text. Locally, the Romanian world became a sphere of divided psyches of a sort that readers of East European writing will be quite familiar with, wherein thoughtful citizens were compelled to lead a double life in which public lip service to the official formulas of the ideological state glossed over inward alienation and non-compliance. This secret defiance could be expressed only in the disingenuous ventriloquism of between-the-lines indirection and Aesopic duplicity: 'I know how to speak without moving my lips…,' she says in a short lyric placed near the close of the narrative sequence, 'as if the wind had uttered / my words'. The effectiveness of *The Triumph of the Water Witch* derives from Ieronim's situating this experience in a sensitive child's precocious apprehension of the unspoken, and literally unspeakable, conditions of her existence, a ripping apart of consciousness like a 'blade…slicing' from within. As the poems move forward in the persona's biography, the glowing miracle of childhood freshness, an archetypal golden age inside a protective family circle, pales into memory with the child's initiation into maturity and adult knowledge. This rite of passage is inextricably, at one and the same time, a descent into some of this century's most malign history.

At the core of Ieronim's vision, thus, the book details a childhood of timeless fairy-tale and magical resonance – 'a world as in any childhood' – inseparable from the quiet wariness of the age and from history's special terrors, a life 'half in flight half in chains', like the wondrous, encyclopaedic Man of the third-to-last poem, with his anatomical overlays.

11

The genesis of the poems is a deliberate act of remembrance that the poet transforms into an attempt to recover the values of a lost way of life elegised in the enlargement and clarity of poetry. The work's episodes and vignettes reimagine this past life, which had fallen from history's grace, as an implicit social model. The book is nostalgic in one sense, therefore, but the impulse from which this nostalgia originates is concomitantly denunciatory, providing scathing testimony to a ravaged spirit of community. At the same time, *The Triumph of the Water Witch* is also intended as a lament specifically for the formerly thriving community of the Transylvanian Saxons which had survived for eight centuries on 'the farthest edges of Europe' before being destroyed in slightly more than four decades by communism's 'slow poisoning'. This sorry chapter among too many similar ones in the book of 20th century European history had as its final turn of events a type of ethnic cleansing through national policy encouraging 'non-Romanians' to emigrate, with West Germany paying a bounty for the repatriation of Germans to their long-ago forsaken homeland (as did Israel, similarly, for many Romanian Jews).

However, despite the prominence and keen flavour of the historical and the mimetic, the fundamental motivation of Ieronim's book is artistic, the crafting of a comprehensive projection of the poet's personal vision. The 'I' of *The Water Witch*, cast overtly in the role of 'guide' to the poems, is more than a voice of retrospection, ironic commentary and moral judgment. It is the basis of a subtly achieved synthesis of varied poetic tonality, lyrical insight, thematically ambitious implication and dramatically charged manipulation of narrative distance. If at some moments conflated with, and at other moments distinguished from, the child's point of view, the autobiographical narrative persona serves, most importantly, to direct attention away from surface specificities and focus much more tellingly on the potential warping and denial of the human spirit in the child's assimilation into her tightly controlled society.

There is, throughout, a dual focus on the world inside and outside the child, and more than a few poems themselves bifurcate into seemingly disparate scenes or psychological elements. These juxtapositions generate, for instance, a bitter poignancy in such episodes as the little girl's objectively absurd grief at Stalin's death in 'The Doctor' or the slyly comic anecdote of childish curiosity in 'At the Pharmacy'. This latter becomes a kind of primal scene of the violation of innocence in the young girl's recognition of the necessity for unremitting caution as wickedness, a 'big dread', a devil 'beneath your ribs'. In recurrent imagery overarching the book's division into individual poems, history's 'great fall' after the war becomes variously conceptualised as, among other metaphors of interior stifling and catastrophe, the encroachment of expedient silence and darkness, the hiding of independent self, a shrivelling or shattering of being, a descent into an everyday hell of mistrust, paradoxically both a drying up and an inundation of human sympathies, and a guillotine about to descend in an imminent death sentence. These powerful figures of speech suggest a sustained intensity, and the forward motion of the embedded narrative is, for the reader, a deeply involving feature of the book's appeal. My reading of the work – as Ieronim's co-translator – is that the interwoven emotional complexities and delineation of character, the social specification and psychological precision, as well as the unrelenting moral alertness, are nonetheless ultimately imbued with a restraint and a perhaps classical poise that express themselves in moments of authenticity, concision and heightened lucidity. Throughout the book there is a projected assurance on the part of the authorial sensibility that her story for itself as an interpretive mirror held up to the century.

Ieronim's supple, responsive prose-poetry medium is part and parcel of her achievement in *The Triumph of the Water Witch*. When I first heard about this book in the course of my visit to her flat ten years ago, Ieronim described her material as forcing her to write in a manner very different from the short, skinny-lined, rather abstract and minimalist poems she had lately been composing. Her new work, she told me, had many elements of fiction, and the subject required the creation of poems that at times would have to work like short stories. This resemblance – or rather, superimposition of modalities – defines what is probably the poems' greatest risk, their inbetweenness of genre. In a potential raised by the oxymoronic name of the prose poem, Ieronim's lengthy paragraph-like lines dare to stretch out into the more leisurely verbal illusion of narrative, but then they suddenly slip back into the intuitive speed and metaphorical (also read: metaphysical) concentration of lyric poetry. Thus the poems offer a multiplicity of pleasures to the reader. And along with the shifts in the writer's voice between immediacy and mediated detachment in relation to the consciousness of the girl she herself once was, this compounding and fusion is made to seem derived from the very nature of the literary form, one which Ieronim herself values with the highest of expectations. An October 1997 e-mail note I received from her, responding to a general question I had posed, most tellingly reveals the magnitude of her faith in the prose poem, She wrote, 'I…think that a synthesis of poetry and prose is what makes the peak of creative writing today, if there were a God to measure creative gold at all, its durable value.' The innovation of the poetry is a strategy of conservation, and the technique, if not immediately glamorous in lexical pageantry and glitter, can be described as richly rewarding in its seeming simplicity.

A note about the title of the book, which invokes a perceptual universe that is part of the 'vast generous air' of these works. The *paparudă*, which we have rendered as 'water witch' to insinuate in English the mark of unnatural power, suggests in ordinary Romanian speech, first of all, a woman in bad taste, with excessive make-up and/or loud, gaudy dress – maybe a vamp or lamia as well. Furthermore, in the seventh poem in the sequence, the one that lends the volume its title, the figure unmistakably points to the post-Second World War Russian woman of the occupation as seen by Romanian sensibilities: a sorceress of both political and demonic potency; a species of savage with painted face and aggressive, masculine demeanour, an insult to nature; and a demiurge of arbitrary time controlled without reference to long-established rhythms of work or diurnal human cycles.

But this ironic phantasm of the triumph of communism and the modern bureaucratic state coexists alongside secondary connotations of a water or rain nymph and hints at layers of age-old custom and ceremony, rituals of fertility and regeneration arising out of traditions from which the villagers, however much dispossessed of land and meaningful work, ultimately could not be orphaned: like the poet's stories of the old ways, 'with drawers – for much, much later'. In an ancient Romanian (and probably pre-Roman) folk practice of the region, in extremely dry weather when the crops were in danger, prepubescent young girls of about ten or twelve (often, in fact, gypsies) would run through the village naked and chanting while covered from head to foot in foliage; the villagers would throw water on them, also giving them a coin or two. This *paparudă* in her verdant, preternatural garb is the imagistic root of the pejorative social applications of the term.

A characteristic strength of Ioana Ieronim's poems in *The Triumph of the Water Witch* is that, by the end of the book, just as with this key expression from the title, the sensory realm of realistic narration and concrete historical reference becomes transfigured. Transfigured, I believe, most of all because of the poet's resolute attention to past and future dimensions inherent in human temporality, as well as to realms of belief, ritual, and myth that speak of, and from, the beyond. Some of the book's most soaring evocations are those of freedom:

physical images, the powerful bulls who, though tied in their stalls, would 'run free upon the face of the earth, /...bathed by the Sun' or the old fortress high above the town, against which the child and her friends 'measure' their breath and being; and intangible, psychological suggestions, the atmosphere of imperishable legend in the school excursion into the woods or the repeated references to words' unfettered, transcendent capacity to disdain frontiers and the Iron Curtain itself as they 'sparkled over time and space'.

The closing few poems in the book are muted, dark with departures, the emigration of the Saxons whose story frames the child's experience and the child's gradual leave-taking from her childhood (in the background, moreover, the relocation of Ieronim's family from Râşnov to Bucharest). However, if distinctly less than hopeful, the concluding action of the narrative is counterbalanced not only by the lyricism which infuses the poet-narrator's realisation of the book's 'sweet-diseased world' but also by symbolic vestiges of another way of life, an older way of seeing that remains congenial to the presence of household spirits, to the living ancestral ghosts who in the next-to-last poem reclaim a rightful place, to the holy. The author's verbal retrieval and celebration of the vanquished world of her girlhood is manifested in a mood of elegiac pastoralism, a poetic lens here refracting illumination from past to future through an aesthetic 'to take care of the words, now', the custodial burden the girl's mother sardonically complains of in 'An Orphan from Tradition'.

Finally, through language, the narrative of the child's struggle to come to terms with the ever starker and more grotesquely diminished here-and-now of her life and the poetry's detailed depiction of her specific, unidyllic historical context, along with her inmost resistance to mental captivity and loss of internal freedom, are together subsumed into a larger, heterogeneous, polysemous world of time conjoined with eternity. This 'invisible' world of 'the timeless essence of shadow the algae of paradise' reinforces human significance and magnifies the poetry's achievement with a generosity like a benediction.

ADAM J. SORKIN

Note on the pronunciation of Romanian letters

This book retains a few characters from the Romanian alphabet not found in English (i.e., English letters with diacritical marks), which are pronounced as follows:

â = like a short i, as in 'win'
ă = short a, as in 'alone'
ş *or* Ş = sh, as in 'rush'
ţ *or* Ţ = ts, as in 'eats'

THE TRIUMPH OF THE WATER WITCH

Journey

I was your guide in the long abandoned places of childhood –
beheld through a pattern of changeless suffering from another life-
     time
words yet unborn cross the prism of the moment, and

all manner of things loom in its transparency, magnified.

Tell me a story, you said.
In lambskin, in the skin of the roe deer, you are smiling.

Tell the story
even though, in its lucid hush, Time streams past an outstretched
     hand.

Annular Eclipse

So I begin my story.
In the perfect void of the moment, within the ring of the eclipse, I
     tell of a static world: a world as in any childhood.
Nothing seems ever to have stirred beyond the threshold worn smooth
     by ancient footsteps. We speak only in whispers.

The child was housed in eternity itself – but all the while history was
     beginning to veer in its great fall.

The electric earth glowed with eerie light.

At the Beginning

The middle of an age adrift, a world at the edge; the crushing war;
　　then convalescence. The world had changed its blood, its garb.
　　You know what they say? They say that after the Transfigura-
　　tion the waters will turn cooler.

In that poverty drought alarm / my parents, so youthful and fresh,
　　departed from Bucharest, crossed the mountains – and stopped
　　in the broad Bârsa plain, where peace seemed to turn in a more
　　generous circle, vast and sheltering.
For them, it was clear, the time to halt had come: their belongings
　　had begun to tumble out of the truck.

Much later, in accordance with their tale, I searched the road for
　　traces of the lion's paws of our chair legs – and it seemed to
　　me I found them.

That Winter

St Nicholas, Christmas, New Year's Eve, Epiphany, St John's Day
– the white echo of the mountains. Surrounded by stone, by
earth – the bears, hibernating. Around limpid pools like eyes
of water, thin paws, warm muzzles leave traces like rays.

My mother had forgotten about all the years she had practised being
'a grown-up' and prepared herself for life. I think she might
even have forgotten the war. She went everywhere smiling,
irreproachable and unstained by sin. She was afraid only of
beholding cripples freaks the lame ugliness hideous scary things,
phantasms which could somehow leave their foul taint on her
unborn child.
The city walls she found too dreary: she would glance at them with
a quick grimace, knock on their closed grey wooden shutters –
and then, like a dark flame, dart away, giggling. She was free
at last, an astonished child in a new world.

In that world all sorts of smells had immeasurable power: they flowed
rippling by you, they slunk furtively with murderous intent, they
gushed out of objects, they changed the contours of everything
that existed.
The most maddening smell was the monster that crept from the door-
way to Trica's shoemaker's shop – from his cans and boxes of
oil and glue and paste and sizing, from his nails and tacks care-
fully sorted in plain view, from the animal hides draped along
the walls, from the room's dark viscera hidden in dismal corners.
Over the shoemaker's shoulder you could see *mămăligă* turned out
of the cooking pot directly onto the wooden plank of the table:
whenever they were hungry, his flock of children grabbed a
hunk of the boiled cornmeal. This was the sole worry of Trica's
woman, that *mămăligă* should never be lacking from this table...
Their children became good craftsmen or professionals. The
most handsome of them was a barber, he got married to a near-
sighted Saxon girl; and one daughter and one son with minds
as sharp as a goblin's became nuclear physicists.
'Rise and shine!' yelled Trica son of Froasa from their doorway one
morning, in that day and time so long ago. It was late. He had
just come from the mayor's office. 'Get up!... Today your father's
become a great man.'

He had been appointed 'Comrade Director' of a factory: he knew how to sign his name.

He never did anything evil to anyone. That's why, people explained, that's why he couldn't keep his place 'up above' for very long. He lived the rest of his life in contentment, fashioning elegant shoes.

*

And there was time. There was time enough.

*

Christmas, New Year's – I should already have *been*, but probably I felt too comfortable under my mother's belt.

My mother's big fear was only that some awful sign some hideous ugliness might pass over her unborn babe, unseen by the gaze of any human eye, unlit by the moon's bright rays.

She carefully averted her eyes from anything repugnant.

New Year's Eve, Epiphany,

St John's Day: the last celebration of midwinter. All the Ions and Ioans would gather to observe their name day at the town hall – and without exception they joined in the Johns' lively round dance of brotherhood (in those years Limping John led the dance). Late in the evening each of them invited a crowd of close friends to their home – where they revelled till daybreak.

My mother danced the night away at the house of my parents' friend John, whose name they gave me – because after the merry-making, after the spirited dancing and the festivity, I at last arrived here in the world (distantly echoing the funny old story about Gargantua and his mother...).

The Fates

We were seated on life's sound that never fades and dies (a kind of
    light which eternally shapes our being, our feelings, bending
    them little by little). All of us. A bridge across the border had
    appeared, a bridge of brass –
a bridge across the earth, of silver.
The breath of Capricorn misted the windows, its tail spreading itself
    throughout the subterranean waters.

My mother had me swaddled tightly, tiny fists
close to my face, as immaculate as on the very first day.
Then
through eyelashes glued shut, through the thinnest, most delicate of
    eardrums,
the Fates made their entrance.
They bore their gifts wrapped in cloud, with three faces.
It turned to night.
Their steps on the cobblestone floor sparked fire, sparked stars.
They had brilliant gowns, the Fates
(here and there, the pearl flowers were beginning to unravel –
but in the pale snow-light, this could not be seen very clearly).

On the far side, Libra, the Scales, in oscillation, trembling
eyes half closed.

The Bârsa Land

In the twilight parting the stalks of wheat like a wave, you sit hidden
   from the world
while poppies burn out with the bright flame of their instant and
   vanish.
In the same earth your slower flame, your very being, coiled within,
   reaches as far as the mountains –
everything flows toward the light.

The sun balances, poised quavering on the ridge of the stone cliffs:
   a divine bird. Out of its hesitation, airy gold floods the visible
   land – and the invisible.

The high wave of Europe breaks against the battlements of the Car-
   pathians. Ship cathedrals sail through the fields lofting beyond
   the arms of young rock, arched in defence, deceptively.

The Triumph of the Water Witch

I was born at a time when the century was breaking in half. More
transparent than the air itself, the arrow crossing above my
slender arms: the god had not yet mapped out my journey –
when tongues of fire flared agony over a wounded earth.
History submerged whole landscapes.
Children would blow delicate soap bubbles down from the roofs.
Children scampered through the streets, propelling hoops with
wire hooks.

A drumroll at the end of the street announced the Triumph of the
Water Witch: the demon's hair permed into wire, her snout
smeared with chemical rouge, a pistol in her boot, a train station
clock on her wrist.
A never-resting star drew the earth out of its orbit. In the arc of the
Carpathians, broken, the sign waited on its knees.
The drum summoned the village to the crossroads – to inform people
of new edicts, new taxes. Other laws, further numbers. In the
end they dispersed back to their homes with eyes cast down to
the ground. On faces beaten by wind, by sun, their thoughts
could not be seen (their necks furrowed by work; younger,
whiter flesh under the collar).

A neighbour, Hajdu the carpenter, looked as if he had eyes of wood.
His lips warped in a long forgotten smile. He returned from
those meetings with slow, solemn tread; each time his shoulders
seemed bent a little lower.

Another neighbour, Herr Geetz, heard that they meant to make him
'a deputy', so he hid in his own house. They elected him any-
way, because so many in the council there heaped praises on
him. Even Colonel Broşteanu described him in glowing terms,
although he didn't have any idea whom he was talking about.

Life's fragrances retreated into the earth. Words into poverty's parched
river-bed. People worked and worked, waiting ('to hope is
almost to live'). Work had never betrayed them, not until now.

Parents and Child

Together they take me in their arms, I am their warm kernel and it
    is good.
They form a circle, they shelter me, they shed light upon me, they
    offer me shade,
They form a circle like two petals, two handles, they flow about me
    in gentleness until they get nearer, they touch, they join:
and I remain at the edge of the world.
I trickle down like a tear
without ever falling.

The void – for me, a cradle.

The moon on one side,
the sun on the other.

*

He embraced me and she embraced me.
In wreaths of joy I shed my leaves until there was only the core of
    cool fire.

Suddenly another understanding, the blade hidden deep within, slicing
    me in two. The silent halves don't ever bleed.

Underneath, the ravenous void howls.

The sun on one side, the moon on the other.

Partisans

Anonymous, they would file across the mountain slopes – attended
    by elves and spirits. Leaflets dropped from the air rotted in
    layers of old leaves.
New-fallen leaves buried deeper and deeper the vain promises of
    the short-wave (Resist! Resist! The Americans are coming!
    The Allies will aid you in your struggle!) – words that spurted
    with difficulty from under the thick reinforced concrete of Radio
    Moscow.
Games played, trinkets thrown upon the Great Sleep.

Time pounding both its fists against the walls – the walls not of stone
    but solid waiting. Hope diluted with water, hope broken, snapped
    like the spine – the arc of the Carpathians, broken.
Eardrums becoming thinner, hearing more tenuous, over the empire
    of the Beast and at the same time over Heaven.

One true sign among all of this: the green mist clinging to the moss
    on the north side.

And exactly the same, exactly as true: death.

Dignity larger-than-life. Lucidity sharper-than-natural. Hence madness.
    The face of the stalked beast.

A candle burns cupped in the hand. You'll never manage to see more
    than that: for there in the depths of the forest, you stand out,
    luminous, others will catch sight of you.
The eye of an angel of man of beast flashed at us, as if one.
Executed. Buried. Every trace covered over, every trace wiped away.

In the cruel funhouse mirrors, thrust before our unwilling faces for
    so long – how shall we ever be able to discern your likeness
    again, and your gift? Who can still know how to make choices?
Maybe only the good God, the One Who has always been too silent.

Your Life Will Be Like This

The solitary snowdrop that pokes up through the eye opened in the
    old snow. Later the beetles of the forest, in pairs, maple seeds
    in a double helix, dogs bound two together after their wedding
    ceremony in the streets (their eyes blank, like the eyes of the
    Venus de Milo).
Kids piglets kittens quivering litters of bunnies golden chicks under
    the brood hen. White mares alongside their black offspring,
    thin gangly foals with knobby knees like children's and legs
    so gawky they have to spread them to touch their muzzles to
    the wet spring grass – their being a toy, a trapezoid vibrating
    in the sight of a smiling God, come down to this valley.
The pale spheres of milk an icon above everything.

*

Mother's first name Maria – the name of suffering. Father's first name
    Mihai – Michael, the name of the militant angel. Your life will
    be like this: nearly nothing that you expected.
Do you of your own free will…? Mihai and Maria Maria and Mihai.

*

Gripped between their knees the lamb sheds its blood drop by drop.
    Once upon a time an obligation, the sacrifice no longer tallies
    in any kind of reckoning. But nobody has stopped doing it.

At the Pharmacy

'But how do they eat?' I asked my mother. Silently, the people in line
   looked at me.
Mama turned her head away. I couldn't see her face.
'Mama!' A pull at her sleeve. 'Tell me, tell me, those up there, how
   do they eat?' My mother, I think, ordered me to shut up. Some
   people near us smiled, their faces directed downward. No one
   uttered a word.
It was the first time I'd asked that question, although I'd wondered
   about it for quite some time: there on the wall of the pharm-
   acy, since they were portrayed with beards disguising their
   mouths, how could they ever eat? Each one separately framed.
   (MARXENGELSLENINSTALIN they were labelled beneath
   them. Anyway, I couldn't read yet.)
Then my mother turned back to me and I caught sight of her face
   once more – my words froze.
But I couldn't understand what I'd done wrong, how I might learn to
   avoid it some other time. When we were by ourselves, Mama
   explained to me, 'You never know who might be near you...'
   My mother's voice drew black furrows across us both. Waves
   of darkness filled the silence.
There's a crossroads where you meet the Devil in the guise of a
   beardless youth, the cunning little old woman, the wicked
   dwarf. A crossroads where the big dread comes out to greet you.
   It has no face. It never eats, but it gets fat. It will be your close
   companion. As heavy as earth. Beneath your ribs. Travelling,
   travelling on your bony shoulders.

*

In his white coat, Mr Pharmacist Mühsam was a closemouthed
   wizard, just a little bit sad. The dome of his head gleaming,
   his face narrow, his fingers thin, his skinny body would glide
   as if an immaterial being among the many wonders of his
   pharmacy.
Mr Mühsam never made a mistake. With scoops he measured powders
   from immense jars, with droppers elixirs from tiny bottles and
   test tubes. There in his old pharmacy, he mixed precious medic-
   aments, poisons in stone mortars. Round lenses framed with
   wire glinted over the eyes of the weary, ever-watchful imp.

Mr Pharmacist Mühsam never never made a mistake.

Though master of so many mysterious tinctures and labels, it was
said he seemed like a church mouse, so poor he was. 'Whatever
good I may do for people, they pay only the doctor. Not me…'
The wing of a butterfly wouldn't have made a more exquisite vibration
than his scales.

Christmas

In the evangelical church they displayed the holy infant every year
at the deepest, darkest moment of winter. In a little red house
lit from within, they showed everything in shadow play exactly
the way it had been: Mary, Joseph and the Magi on their knees
gaze into the manger, the cattle warm the child with their breath,
as if a calf of their own.
The little house had its place under the fir tree that towered way up
to the decorated vault. On both sides of the church in long
wooden balconies, boys and girls, dressed for the holiday,
their cheeks rosy, kept watch over the candles so the tree
wouldn't catch on fire. Each was armed with a long thin pole:
when a wick flared high among the branches and ornaments,
one of the boys, his face blushing deeper red with bashful self-
importance, would snuff the flame.
The eyes of the children became radiant with the flickerings on the
fir tree. But the grown-up men, the grown-up women…how
did they look at things?
Their voices ascended to the arches, resonating in unison, the voices
swirled among the columns like bare trees, trees like signs.
The organ swelled from depths far below, the organ spiralled
down from on high.
In rows on the wooden benches, all the world sang, people curling
further within, worming into themselves. Earthly beings and
heavenly beings. Hope and a tear between worlds.
At the end, gifts: apples biscuits shining gilt walnuts little glittering
goodies. Voices caroling, the organ soaring above everybody.
Then people scattered in every direction.

You would leave but the music kept you company (oh gladness, goodness) beyond the walls of the church to the narrow streets, far into the distance. The voice of the organ permeating the gossamer of your bodily fabric, air and flame.

I was with my grandmother. ('They make it so nice, too... Do you see how they prepared a gift for you, as if you were among their own children?' She was whispering to me as we walked home in darkness. 'Did you tell them *thank you*?') The snow scrunched under our feet.

My jaw was stiff, clenched with emotion. Everywhere I turned my eyes – bright windows. 'Think he's been...he's been to ours... to our house?'

Usually on Christmas Eve while the two of us were at the German church, Father Christmas would come with the tree and gifts, but he had to hurry away to visit other children. Faithfully, he forgave my mistakes – year after year he was kind. Every year he also left behind a number of duties for me.

Our tree was nice, the nicest. And Father Christmas never forgot the white angel and the little stars and the funny clown as fat as a barrel. And the Hess chocolates wrapped in crinkly coloured foil. You couldn't eat those any more: Father Christmas had been keeping them since the time of the war and each year there were fewer.

Ida

I could never hear when she opened her little gate in the ivy-covered wall. How she froze me with her eyes, with her dry voice like crushed stone. Near Ida's shadow, black like a black bat, I gave a leap – my heart throbbed darkly and blinded me. Through the air suddenly filled with flames I would manage to get home inside my own gate.

Ida's garden – the forbidden place.

You were only allowed to pass through one end of it on a long narrow board, perpetually slick (you would have thought a northern territory breathed between the walls of her garden, it was so cool and damp).

But on the path, the deepest silence descended upon you (each place has its singular voice of silence) – and then I'd set off for the sand alley between the straight, flowering hedgerows.

I didn't touch leaf or tree. Halfway, I usually turned around: sometimes at the faint crack of the red currant twigs, or the whish of a wingbeat of wind.

Everything there belonged to Ida – Ida, soul of a witch.

If there were the slightest sign, a flutter, a stir, I'd run madly back. Nevertheless it happened sometimes that she caught me (you never knew when she would come gliding noiselessly through her little gate in the ivy)…just when I had arrived at the heart of her garden, on the grass (oh, the drowsy-scented cradle) beneath the walnut tree.

Here I could see the snowdrops sprouting, how they warmed the snow in circles. How overnight they vanquished the armour of the ice crust: what rustlings and secret happenings occurred under the translucent white mane! I would kneel in the warm snow, I would bring my face near.

'You should never, oh no, never stay awake the whole night till dawn,' children whispered. 'That's what Ida did…that's why now she's so lonely and so loony.'

In their unknown bed, lost in Ida's garden, grew the most beautiful lilies of the valley in the entire world.

Ida was a widow, the widow of…of whom?

The wife of darkness.

She had a handsome young son as handsome as the sun itself – Horst.

Once a year he'd come to see her, and

then she bustled about as sprightly as a young girl, she flew through doorways, how the pots rang while she prepared his food.

She laughed and laughed with her voice of stone and shade, totally transformed.

But soon he went off to the mountains, soon he set out again into the wide world, and

then night after night she would cry, twisted tight like a gnarled root – until she settled back into her old channel.

Epiphany

In winter my grandmother put on her big black fur collar, so big you couldn't even see her fair and kindly face. Before leaving the house, I would tramp in a circle as her fur coat ballooned about her. I stretched my hands high up and caressed the tail of the fox like petting a cat. Grandmother never minded.

On Epiphany, the cold was so bitter that the snow under our boots squeaked with dryness. Silvery-blue steam blossomed in the air when we breathed.

People would come out of their arched gates, framed by the depths of their walls. All of us on our way to church.

At the river, with colourful banners, a big crowd had gathered, singing. As we approached, the scene looked like a painting stretched along the water. When we joined the crowd, I was squeezed snugly among the people's warm clothes, I could only look up at the blue-violet sky as through a tunnel – and the plumes of their warm breaths. The priests spoke, everybody sang, I felt the buzz of their bodies. I would cross myself whenever everybody else did, fearful of making a mistake. ('These people here sing differently from us nearer the Dâmboviţa River,' Grandmother murmured.)

At the end we scattered to the winds on the way home – you would have said it was like a great thaw.

My grandmother and I were very merry together. Proudly she greeted people in the street ('Good appetite!' 'Many happy returns!' 'Long life!'). I never left the folds of her fur coat. Her high, glossy patent leather boots were the shiniest anywhere, really.

The Crown

In Braşov, the former City of the Crown – Kronstadt – Stadt Kronn
– Stalin City, heavy salvers and clasps with aristocratic coats
of arms and symbols of power fecundity faith – masked among
a hodgepodge of cast-iron kettles broken pots rusty locks empty
frames candles toothless clocks with coy nymphs on their faces
old things crammed higgledy-piggledy in the same shop win-
dow so as to lose the last vestiges of their nature (an hourglass
in the muzzle of a dog sleeping under a thick coverlet of dust)
– for sale for a handful of tinny coins in a world altogether,
absolutely new.

History refracted through the young parents' being.

The clock in the Kremlin, toothless likewise, would strike as a sign
that a mistake had been made: oh, the mistakes of 'the working
class' do not have to be stared at straight in the eye. At night,
in secret, guards and bulldozers surrounded 'The Father', at
night a tractor pulled to the ground his massive trunk with the
military cap on its head. His stiff arm that had been extended
everywhere throughout the country struck the earth.
Drops of poison in everyone's bones had descended from father to
son, from leaves to the ground.

Walls and Life

We were living in Ida's house, which had been designed for another kind of life. A large door separated us from her: within its deep frame were suitcases and clothes piled to the ceiling, hidden behind the curtain – this was my territory of secrets and fright.
Muffled by layers of darkness, Ida's life could still be heard.

On the other side of the house, there was the second courtyard, 'the work yard', with an enormous shed and another row of houses – these belonged to Ida. It was there that they set up the Veterinary Clinic: a semicircle of glass as big as a wall led you to the main hall, bathed in light, with massive equipment, with instruments and glittering metal boxes in glass cabinets on heavy oak tables.
From morning to night people brought their livestock for my father to examine in that courtyard.
Once a year the horses from all the villages and the mountains would assemble.
Hundreds of horses filled the street for hours while more and more arrived, until at last the sun slowly sank toward setting and hazy flames flickered through their manes.

This is what they decided to do with Ida's household after the war – because she lived by herself in her house designed for another kind of life.

Master of the Mountains

'*Don't say anything* in anyone's presence. Don't speak when the child
    might hear,' my mother whispered. 'Don't speak out loud. You
    never know what might happen. And leave *those things* be,
    because who knows what can happen to you for no reason, as
    it has to others...just for listening to some idle chatter...'
But in the evening when my father began searching for broadcasts
    and the short waves shrilled (in the air catastrophe was shat-
    tering the world, heart-stopping cascades), mother was ready
    to bring her chair nearer, her knitting in her lap, waiting.

Father was Master of the Mountains. He was the strongest. Free in
    his every way. Harmonious. And he was able to laugh with his
    whole being. He was able to laugh there at the tattered edge of
    sorrow and astonishment.

Alarm gathered between parentheses. Questions about evil ransomed
    by his healing voice.
Everybody trusted him. Not even the nastiest dog would lunge at
    him to bite. His speech could measure the most fitting distance
    for everything in the world.
The first Tamer must have resembled my father.

I do not know how much others were able to learn from his know-
    ledge, but he worked hard with very little help for the good of
    animal-kind throughout the villages of the Bârsa plain, the
    many sheepfolds and farms and food factories. He looked after
    the cattle at so many households, each domestic animal like a
    close relative in a diminished family – the mute sustaining god.
Father was master over all this. Always he'd come back from his
    work smiling, always with the scent of distance in his hair, in
    his clothes, on his face.
In the afternoon he drank his coffee: was it the same coffee filling
    the same cup, the cup dipped in silver like a petal? I'd stay
    nearby him so I could breathe the delicate steam – and later,
    I'd tell Father where the hands of the kitchen clock had reached,
    the clock as old and big as the clock in the railway station.

Friends in Need

On that night, during the summer of '48, my mother would tell me,
we had a dinner party at our house. It was late. Somebody
knocked at the door. They were looking for Herr Stamm.
Stamm owned the knitting mill here on our street. When he
came back to our dining-room – it's as if I can see him now –
he was as white as that wall. He returned to the table. Everyone
remained silent. At last, his breast heaved and he drew in air.
He was calming down. A man who worked at the mill had told
him that the Nationalisation would take place on the follow-
ing day. This had been expected, but… 'Take what you can,'
the man had advised him. 'No, no.' 'At least some clothes for
the wife, Herr Stamm. These are hard times.' '*No!*'
And nobody could talk him into leaving the party (through his mind
various strands unravelled, the long roads of his young man-
hood, the nights of labour). Until dawn he remained here with
us, unspeaking.
In the morning he handed over the keys and the accounts in perfect
order. For some time he went on helping to manage, until others
could learn.
'Where on our street, Mama?' I would ask again. 'But I've told you
so many times – where the Toy Factory is now.'
I could scarcely believe it had been any other way, that inside the big
dusty gates forever flung open as if they'd never known an
owner – right there in the yard full of shavings, splinters and
sawdust into which children were not allowed to go – they
had not always made coloured balls and blocks and wheels
and little duckies and miniature trucks with doors you could
open, entirely of wood, like each of us children had.
Once more Mother was counting the stitches on her needles, in a
loud whisper.
When they learned to make everything work and keep the records
in perfect order, she resumed telling the story, they banished
Uncle Stamm… Do you understand? They no longer had any
need of him. Do you understand? So they forced him to go live
somewhere else.
About a month later, we went to visit them in the little town where
for a flat they had been given a *cellar*, a real cellar with an
earthen floor and tiny windows up at street level. We found
them bearing up well, in good health and spirits, both him,

Stamm, and Aunt Annie. In the neighbourhood they'd already come across some friends from their childhood, who like themselves had been resettled to that place.

In that cellar, with its cave-like rooms, they had first put down a layer of rushes and straw – and then, on top of that, their Persian rugs and some of their nicest things – the Viennese furniture their curtains the inherited silverware their heirlooms.

A miracle, as in *1001 Nights* – they had transformed that cellar.

(At the end Aunt Annie's eyes glistened with tears; she hid them behind her glasses… 'At least I managed to make a *home* like we were used to – but it's so dark and damp. And they make him to do heavy labour. He digs ditches. One of his hands has started to get stiff and numb – though he won't admit it. And one finger has started to curl from the cold, from the spade. Is this only until he gets used to it?… Come to see us again – if you're not too afraid. If before tomorrow and the day after, everything doesn't get worse and worse.')

Herr Stamm, oh, he was such a striking figure, intelligent charming graceful, he was warm-hearted, he had a sense of humour.

She was a silent grey-green partner, behind her glasses a bit obscured in her shallower waters. Weak currents circulated through her transparent blood.

'Well, that's the way some pairs of living creatures are,' Father added, with a smile, 'the brilliant plumage on the male, and the splendour.'

Once before the war, when they were young, while they were strolling in Vienna, a forward young girl (how she dazzled with the rich colours of life, as they used to say) had thrust Aunt Annie aside and clutched Stamm's arm: 'With me beside you, you'd look so much better…'

*

And…and…?

Oh? Oh, yes. In accordance with Aunt Annie's wish, they departed for Germany. But there, fairly soon, she died.

He is rich. He keeps travelling – forever running away, away from himself.

Today he may be a traveller still. The stiff fingers of his left hand permanently gripping the handle of an imaginary spade.

The Measure of Time

People and things reappeared on the dial of the days, after hours of
air water fire earth. Tower clocks of leaves and wind. After
the muffled resonance of the organ and flutes. Evening shadows
across bridges.
The movement of the world balanced on the shoulders of a child.

There were days measured in the click of knitting needles. Or in the
rivulet of trickling wool. There were days ablaze with joy. Or
charred slowly by grown-ups' tears. There were nights when
my forehead felt brushed by a ring of gold, by the rising of
the new moon.
Unstained by sin, evening returned in the company of a herd of cattle.

We were together, and then we were not – each of us in keeping with
our own allotted enumeration. Under everybody's ribs, a clock
with turning gears: you rarely could predict the direction of
their cycles, their speed.

In the middle of August every year my father, the first herald, led
my brother and me by the hand to the end of the street to show
us the new snow on the mountains.
Another year is passing, he would say.
My eyes transfixed by the white fields, which seemed closer and
closer, I would hang onto my father's hand, my vibrant body
echoing with the joy of the snow. On the street the shadows
grew longer and longer.

My Friends' House

Since they were poor, you could come in whenever you wanted to.
Whenever you wanted, you could taste from the cooking pots,
drink from the water bucket with a ladle, rummage about in
the drawers, the corners.

Their entrance room, nevertheless, you'd hardly ever enter. There
you spoke in a whisper, the wooden blinds always closed, the
furniture dark brown and old. In the middle of the room, hang-
ing low from the big table, stretched sheets of noodle dough
shone white, draped almost to the floor.
Silence. The house gave signs.
There were embroideries on little tables and in the china cabinet,
framed portraits on silver stands... Under the dark bedspread
covering the bed with its spiral posts, luminous ruffles glowed
from the shadows.
On the wall – a picture in a broad wooden frame: a little girl sat, her
face turned toward us, a bit sad but smiling. 'She's our big sister,'
explained Misch, Rita and Günther. 'She was pretty and good.
She died a little child.' The girl in the picture always looked
as if she wanted to stand up from her chair the next moment.

Silent, we passed back across the threshold, we drew ourselves from
there with difficulty – and suddenly we burst into brightness.
We chased each other out through the kitchen / the aroma of a pie
baking for later on.
Then the scent of hay from the hay attic spreading downward like a
mantle, the oven for *baumstritzel* set in the wall, beneath the
attic. Ah, *baumstritzel*, 'the boot', the best pastry in the world.
The cloying rankness of the manure heap for the field hit into us,
cutting like a sharp knife and making us wince
then the garden, the grass crushed by our running, the fallen apples
juicy, the taste of redcurrants, of sorrel
the fence of long, weathered boards: a little door could be unpinned
from its rusted hinges, you could drag it along, softly, over the
weeds and beyond the millrace – the rocky bank (the rocks big
and white and jagged, young, fresh rubble from the mountain),
the rush of rippling water, its many braided ropes like snakes
and the white plash –
the stream-bed shimmered toward another realm: thousands of colours
and faces played in the depths, fixed within the smooth frame
of dark wood. You could see their chase, without being able
to touch it or join in.

Neighbours

'Any visitor can zhow up, I won't care,' Frau Mitzi laughs, toothless.
'I'll put him at table and give him good zoup, with noodles: I
boil one more ladleful of water in the pot and that does the
trick! Noodles I've got plenty of, throughout the whole house
I've hung sheets of dough to dry…not a zoul dare come near
them, zo help him! For us these noodles will be enough, enough
for an entire year.'

Frau Mitzi is in a good mood today, she laughs with her small voice,
the hoarse voice of someone hard-working and silent. 'Any
visitor can zhow up, not just Herr Gagesch – for that one, that
one comes always always, like a neighbour / and Michael,
poor Michael, he throws him such hateful glances – he's con-
sumed with jealousy…against Gagesch most of all. But tell
me, zo, can I turn the man away? How can I?'

Old man Gagesch… (How old was that old man? His neck was the
most wrinkled in the entire world.) He was keeper of the bulls.
A ruddy bull's head was mounted high on the front wall of his
house, the sweeping, soaring horns yellowed by age.

It was very dangerous to enter the gate at Gagesch's. In the shadowy
stables with bars over the little windows, the bulls, each tied in
his narrow place, bellowed snorted butted against the massive
timbers. They were nervous, pawing, tormented; their captive
strength could be felt pulsing through the walls.

There was no beast more dangerous than a bull anywhere around our
village. When they wanted to lead such a colossus to another
village nearby, they'd have to tie one of the biggest and heaviest
carts behind his back.

Savage, deaf, and blind with fury, with humiliation, the animal would
listen to no commands, obey no cudgel or whip – violently,
he'd thrash about from side to side: four oxen in yoke could
hardly succeed in dragging him forward.

He would have willed himself to rise from the ground into the air like
a whirlwind, everybody and everything with him, to destroy
them totally, and

run free upon the face of the earth,
free
in his story bathed by the Sun.

Misch

Misch had to touch things with his enormous hand: his face fair, his
    eyes always perplexed.
Any question, after some delay, he'd respond to very slowly. Because
    in his mind he had to touch things bit by bit, with his fair hands.
There was something delicate in his smile like a skittish unicorn,
    something awkward and loving. An Irreality.

Much later, when he was as big as a grown man, they gave him glasses
    …And then he became another person.

*

That summer he built himself a little cabin where he lived for some
    time sheltered from the elements and secure,
and around the border just under the ceiling he painted in sweet cal-
    ligraphy the prayer of his nest to God – who now could see
    his writing much more clearly with glasses:
ÄCH BÄN E SAKS DES STUW ÄS MENJ – AS HÄRRGOTT MEG AS
    GNEDISCH SENJ
In this small room a Saxon You'll find – Lord, grant me mercy and
    be kind.

The Deaf Man

He'd had typhus in childhood – his speech could be understood only
   by his family and near neighbours. His gaunt clenched face
   was a painful sign from deep inside you'd rather not look at.
   He came from a small, poor village – from a family who in
   former times had been proud and well-off: they bought their
   damaged son a bride.

'I would of went to Australia as a young man together with my
   brother and I'd have myself a lot of herds, a lot of sheep – like
   him… It's a lifetime since we heard from each other. And I
   can't get a fair shake this way…no way, can't accomplish
   nothing. Not those children not my woman, they too don't
   seem to heed me. What's gonna become of children who haven't
   learned no respect?

'For I understand more than people like to believe. I ain't sunk so
   low down. But there's no order no longer.

'There's none. None.' His face screwed up in bitterness like a brittle,
   dry shell. Tall bony ageless (the age of pain) Michael stood in
   silence among his ghosts.

'So many blab on and on to me: "You've got it so much better, Michael,
   because you're deaf…you're spared hearing about all them bad
   things. Don't you see what this world's turned into, Michael?
   So much better for you, Michael. Michael, you live in peace
   and quiet. Michael, Michael, Michael…"

'Peace and quiet? When I can always hear noises, a tumult, never-
   ending, always in my head – terrible avalanches torrents of
   water senseless voices summoning – and they don't give me a
   moment to myself, no moment, not least in my sleep. At this
   very second I can hear 'em, thousands of voices, lamenting, a
   vortex mourning up to God Himself. As if I who's without
   hearing am not punished enough…as if it's not enough of a
   punishment. As if I'm forced to listen to everybody's misery
   and moans. The hullabaloo of the entire creation.

'So I wander out to the road to talk to someone. Talk. Just to jabber.'
   Michael wrenches syllables from the depths with great diffi-
   culty, he crushes dry crackling words against the walls of his
   mouth.

'Yes, yes…no order. There's none. No order no longer.'

An Orphan from Tradition

When your feet already grown too large get frozen in the same pair
of boots
when you shiver in the same worn-out coat from autumn through
next spring
when you can hardly find anything in the kitchen cupboard to spread
on your black bread – that means your parents have lost so
much that they have started losing the memories as well
: Well, who can know anything about the feast days now? The old
people knew a different age and time.
And there are no occasions to use some of the words any longer,
either – of course they get forgotten. 'So we're also supposed
to take care of the words now!! Why do you tease people with
so many questions, my child?! Go and learn what you need to,
but do it on your own.'

From the costumes of the old days, only a few parts have been kept.
But for Confirmation you'll have to have the complete outfit. It's
lucky that the grocery's had some flowered ribbon delivered:
including edelweiss, do you hear, with blue and black. You
can sew it on the fabric. And, if you look at it from far enough
away, it will appear embroidered by hand.

Yes. When you've lost too much, you'll be an orphan even from your
traditions.

The Century Was Breaking in Half

At the edge of the field, the cattle snorted and pawed in terror, press-
ing together, as they were herded to the slaughterhouse. These
beings, driven to their fate, let loose their voices. Their bellow-
ing rolled across the fields, taking refuge in the mountains.

Massive halves of animals were hanging by one leg from nickel
hooks built into the porcelain:
then the image of the interior – in clear focus, at last.
The blood and offal drained away down a cement ditch.
Men covered in rubber from head to foot were the masters here. They
were able to hoist whole lifeless animals on their back. They
drank fresh blood from a mug, and they feasted on the tenderest
meat, roasted in the courtyard over an eternally burning grill.
Although they were busy all the time, although they never listened
to a word of it – the National Radio, turned up very loudly,
talked at them day and night. It was going to vanquish them.

Works and Days

I stood at a wary distance watching the huge cast iron cauldron in which my mother was boiling soap in the courtyard. My mother was arranging it just so, was casting spells on it; she would grasp it at full boil and lift it from the soot-blackened tripod over the fire, then lower it to the white limestone pebbles to cool.

Soon the soap could be seen starting to coagulate in a yellowish layer; a thick dark liquid remained beneath. ('What is it you're looking for here?' I could hear their voices. 'You're not to touch…'). Inside that kettle, a poisonous brown eye.

My mother had poured in caustic soda from a glass jar where the poison grew into crystals that clinked as if frozen, like in the land of the Snow Queen where the only word you could not make was *Eternity*.

On the belly of the jar my father had drawn a death's-head and crossbones (every once in a while you heard about somebody in the village, a child or a big person, who had drunk some by mistake – it was awfully serious – and you never knew…).

I was frightened by this. It was a mystery to me how my mother – with her silken hands and her pretty rings, her dainty hourglass waist, her fair face – could come so close to the fire, to all kinds of boiling liquids sharp edges poisons various sorts of dangers, splashing streams of hot melted lard, simmering tomato sauce, fires under enormous stew pots, spattering drops of preserves that would burn you. My mother held fire in her hands, or so it looked sometimes.

Even after I waited and waited to taste the pink foam of rose preserves from a saucer, it was still warm, but my mother stretched her arms out and stirred the intensely bubbling core of the boiling.

In my mother's quick motions glimmered the powers of a witch. 'Go, go and play,' she told me.

Maybe Mama liked it…this world of dangers? I sat on a box, nearer the door. 'Well, you can look on from there, so you'll know how, too, when you're in your own home, after you've become big!'

Me, big? Oh, no. Never.

A curtain lowered itself over my eyes, visions of foxes, words that
        meant to snatch me in their claws,
burning rivers, the fold of a dress in flames, knives biting deep into
        the hand. No, no! I opened my eyes.
Like a flame herself, my mother went on with her work, farther away,
        while
from my cool river-bank I stared at her, a goddess: of fire / of danger…

NO!

Arranging the Wardrobe

There was no greater joy than 'arranging the wardrobe' when Mama
brought out everything from deep in the most hidden corners –
she would sit and stare, sometimes reminisce in a loud voice.
She would smile at nothing.
Now and then she cried (just a little, a little, I didn't quite have time
to realise).
Again the bracelets brooches rings I'd almost forgotten: they seemed
to be different in the light / while I was scraping my knees
against jagged stones on the mountain, here they were, in
cool shade, asleep on their silken beds.
And bonbon boxes... Capşa Zamfirescu Suchard...filled to the top
with letters; small boxes like little sanctuaries among ancient
bed sheets with serpentine embroidery – you never got to use
them, for they 'tore all by themselves' from age on the shelves.
The warm woollen stockings for 'any eventuality'.

Once there was a big sorting of the medicines from before the 'Arm-
istice'. They were so beautiful, such as I'd never seen: glittering
labels like ornaments for the Christmas tree; diaphanous pills
translucent crystals pale liquids nearly transparent (German
and Swiss, they told me – you used to find them everywhere
then. 'Eh! It's better, though, that we didn't need them...').
They were afraid that someone might get poisoned because the
medicines were very old, so they threw them into the fire of
the big stove that heated the dining-room.
Boom! – a loud explosion blew off the stove's red clay top. Above
the stove as high as the ceiling, a whirlwind of soot; and a
rain of earth and soot covered us. But the stove, which had
been constructed by the finest German craftsmen, in another
life, stood firm.

There was no greater joy than 'arranging the wardrobe' from time
to time, when the mystery of things had deposited a film of
scented oxide the timeless essence of shadow the algae of
paradise.

Another Season

Aunt Edith is busy knitting. I'm crocheting blue eyes out of silk: a chain...as long as...as long as the earth. Uncle Fritz reads us a story for grown-ups.

Uncle Fritz and Aunt Edith understand all sorts of things. They are smiling. They often sit in silence for a long time between the lines.
I myself understand, though maybe half.

Outside – white winter. Outside – the field, lonely, bruised by darkness. Deep in the earth, drowsy, numb lives, awaiting another season.

Rembrandt van Rijn smiles at us, toothless and old, from the upper bookshelf.
A light streams upon us.

Mother's Crying

Mother's crying shattered my cloudless mood in a flash. Her shoulders suddenly seemed caved in, her posture broken, her face cast down to the ground, unfamiliar. Her tears put out the sun. Flooded the night's power. No defense existed – the enemy stayed deep inside you, as if hidden in an abandoned well.

*

Our neighbour had disappeared from among us (they arrested him last night...have you heard have you heard? they whispered, their faces in mourning) and my godfather was nowhere to be seen any more (they've taken Mr Doctor, whatever could he have done? they took him at night like thieves, we received so much good from him and they dared to take an innocent man, they'll be punished, the wheel will turn, won't it, oh, won't it?) but now the wheel has been forced against its nature to skid into the valley.

Mother's soundless crying for those who would never show up again. Where? where? Has anyone learned something about him... Gherla Jilava Aiud Călăraşi, cellars secret rooms re-education a life sentence detained without trial water up to their knees in rags in snow in sewer ditches in solitary confinement with rats. Făgăraş Sighet Baia Sprie Piteşti, hunger humiliation murder continual reassignment finally set free with excuses (oh, of course, we know you're innocent but now you can't expect to find any type of employment you have to understand us, *you* have been *there*...and listen, no talking about it, keep your mouth buttoned shut!).

A handful of words pass from man to man among the poor creatures come from *there*. A vanquished land...a Russky pashalic (my parents whispered this between them) such has become our fate...the deepest of mines cells reeds rottenness.

Nevertheless one day he will open the gate to his house, one day his shadow will glide across the windows (happy pained anxious shy), one day he will pass softly over all of us, his shadow most luminous one day.

Sunday Morning

On Sunday, in winter, when all of us would go out together
we dressed in our heaviest overcoats. Even Father, instead of his light,
    warm work coat, put on his dark blue winter overcoat as if a
    suit of armour – and he could no longer move freely as before.
Before we went out, we kept brushing each other, and we'd run a
    damp palm over the coats.
'Oh, these heavy, dark fabrics…any mote of dust in the air, the least
    filament of lint…'

We kept shifting about with straight shoulders, checking each other
    a last time. Then – ready for the holiday (it looked as if we had
    sticks instead of arms instead of necks) –
we crossed the threshold
with a smile on our faces, and transformed breathing.

The Ball

In February there was always the Ball. Nobody from our school
    ever missed it. In the big hall decorated with fir branches we
    would dance the polka the waltz the tango. (Those dances
    requiring patterns of steps were always the nicest!) Whenever
    we changed partners, crushed together in the smaller hall, the
    Blasmusik on stage quickly summoned us back with a march.
    We'd return in new pairs, and in pairs we'd promenade around
    the empty space in the middle, winking at our friends, catching
    our parents' eye.
Our families would watch, seated along the walls in a crowded circle,
    a wreath woven of love. Minute by minute as time hurried
    on, our tight curls and slicked-down hair loosened from their
    constraints. In the brass band were mature men and a handful
    of younger ones, two or three home on leave from the army
    just for the Ball. Here they lorded it over us, with trombones
    trumpets horns saxophones gold and glittering, with cymbals
    and drums.

At the end it wasn't easy to persuade our teachers and the other grown-ups to let us stay a little longer, only one polka more.

All too soon we had to depart, dressed in our Sunday clothes – wrinkled and creased. We'd take as much time as we could to make our way home; for a long while afterwards children in groups filled the snow-covered streets with their cheers, their games and pranks.

The grown-up people remained for their Fancy Dress Ball. It was growing late. The night full of signs, transparent.

On the following day they told us their stories – and at school we collected the stories among us.

...Frau Erna chose to dress as a housemaid, did you hear about that? Not a soul recognised her. Tied from her belt dangled all the scrub brushes that she had. A stained apron. And she went around with a long feather-duster for dusting ceilings. She changed her walk, too... She was wonderful. Wonderful. Horrible.

But 'the moon'? How about 'the moon'? (The moon was always a paper lantern rigged up on a wire to cross the entire room lengthwise.) The moon? It went very v–e–r–y slowly – and in its sweet-sweet-glow only those in love danced. 'And we two, I with Edith' – he'd been telling me his story with an amused arch of his lips, Uncle Fritz, a glint in his eye and in the best of humour. 'But what were you?' I couldn't help but ask him. 'I? Oh, a sultan, everyone knows that.' / Yes, this same moon also rose once beneath the ceiling and then set, for us children. But it wasn't fun; it was still daylight outside.

Aunt Edith and Uncle Fritz

Uncle Fritz had had factories, properties. Studies in England and years of his youth in France, in Italy. Then he came back to his country and took his father's place in managing their wealth. He did his duty: without enthusiasm, but with easy grace.

At the moment of the 'settling of accounts' after the war, they were astonished to discover he had no enemies. They didn't even succeed in finding a willing false witness, not a single one.

He hadn't gone to war. He read enormously. He entertained. He had a playful soul. He liked women with long, luxuriant tresses.

He would wear a ring with a reddish square stone, engraved with the coat of arms of his family: a fine signet like a spider's silk filaments. He was without descendants, the last of his family. He had not engraved his name on the thinnest branches of his genealogical tree.

Right after the war he married Aunt Edith, a recent widow. She had had the most beautiful hair in Transylvania, the glory of grand balls. When she rode in equestrian competitions, it was difficult for her to keep her thick blonde hair under her riding helmet. She had given birth to three daughters and a son: when her son was born, Aunt Edith received from her husband the gift of a full-blooded white Arabian stallion.

Preparing the Christmas tree in their family occupied a month – in a big salon which they kept locked. Children conspired in vain to find a way in. On that magic evening when the doors were thrown open, there were gifts and surprises for everybody down to the gardener, the scullery maids, the apprentices. And the favourite dog had a bone tied with ribbon to the tree's branches.

'…Look here…as you can see in this photo…' Aunt Edith would open the album with the gilt monogram. 'There they are, my grandparents, photographed on New Year's Eve with a fat suckling pig on the table, which they customarily served – the suckling pig with a fork and knife stuck into its back and, in its snout, a flower. The two of them stand there so proud and so dutifully erect, because the photographer told them they had to remain stiff as stakes for several minutes. He stayed hidden under the black cloth of his camera – like a scarecrow, with a hand in the air. The youngest children were terrified to peek at him.'

'Here, is this the grandmother who wrote *The Transylvanian Cook-book*?' I asked, with the image of that book in my mind: the same gold imprint stamped into its worn-out black leather cover. 'No...she's the one who liked to dance, to go to the theatre. That book was written by her mother: she gathered recipes for a lifetime, she crisscrossed hundreds of villages in a speedy victoria that was just hers. She also collected formulas for folk remedies. It was only in her old age that she finally was satisfied and gave the *Cookbook* to a master typographer in Braşov.'

'...And then?... And then?' I'd ask endlessly, trying to keep the story forever open. Aunt Edith had never spoken that much in her life, told so many stories, as in those years when, teaching me German, her native language, she distilled her life into words, with a few other lives close to her, and presented them to me.

Stories with drawers – for much, much later.

'And then?'

'Eh?'... It turned out that one year, in February, so people wouldn't recognise her behind her mask at the balls and revelries – they'd last round the clock, days and nights – Aunt Edith had cut her thick tresses and left her hair short and wavy. She won the prize, of course: nobody could recognise her.

The war was near.

'And then?... What came next?'... 'You want to know? Then it was over and done with.'

'And after that, what came after that?'... At that point Aunt Edith would repeat one of the older stories: the gods, likewise, enjoy hearing the same tale over and over again I-don't-know-how-many-times. To which, in the meantime, a little secret gets attached, a tiny new branch...

*

When Uncle Fritz took Edith for his wife, she had recently been freed from prison. (They'd put her there instead of her husband, who no longer was. They'd put her there instead of her daughter Edith, who had departed abroad.) From the moment she was imprisoned, Aunt Edith remained nearly bald. She always wore a turban. It suited her. Uncle Fritz adored her.

Never for an instant did I see them as old: they rambled side by side through the woods; at the swimming pool in the Valley of the Old Fortress they were the best swimmers. Suddenly you'd be able to see, in the glimmer of a smile, a flash of childhood.

Sometimes, between them, I didn't find any space for my own love – there was that invisible wall, as happens at times between child and parents. When you learn that your place is outside the gates. Outside their fortress of two. You see it. You forget... Between here and the wide world, there are also landscapes of walls for you.

*

For a long time, in truth, I was their daughter, too. We stayed suspended in the warm crystal of a freezing history. In spite of everything we abided together until it was very late in the day – when everyone slipped into another frame.

I was, in truth, their child. Then, by the will of that mysterious clock, I could be their child no longer.

Words

When I'd come back from school a trip or playing and some improper
   word popped up in my stories, Uncle Fritz was quick to des-
   cribe for me from what kind of person that word had got stuck
   on my tongue – from what kind of distorted sentence what
   kind of colourful embroidered decoration on what kind of
   kitchen wall: an interloper, a parasite, now contemplated
   between us for a long time, transformed into the hero of a
   commedia –
and I'd laugh and be ashamed that I hadn't been able to recognise
   and vanquish the treacherous word.
But in the very next moment Uncle Fritz changed the scene: at a
   sign he assembled ranks of smartly dressed words, in tie and
   tails, with thin refined smiles... He was able to play like that
   in several languages, no less than in Romanian; he paraded
   hosts of words across our frontiers without paying duties; while
   looming from horizon to horizon, the Iron Curtain absorbed
   every echo. (Waves with the infrequency of a century washed
   below, through phreatic waters.)
The being of his words sparkled over time and space as in some
   wake resonating from Finnegan into the deepest extremity of
   the Carpathians – mirrors which contained everything life-
   size, but much more luminous.

*

And there was a strange festivity, the table forever laid in the closing
   words of a fairy-tale and stretching endlessly to the margin of
   time.

Holidays

In winter and spring, at holiday time, neat little packages circulated
  throughout Transylvania; a pair of hand-knitted socks, multi-
  colour gloves made of leftover yarn, a pot-holder of flowered
  cloth,
a napkin embroidered with a dainty blue cross by a schoolgirl, a
  muffler, a fur cap, a lace shawl – or perhaps a box filled with
  biscuits (which, it's well known, will be much better if you
  wait to eat them later) – or some pie, if the distance was fairly
  short
: with love and best wishes for Aunt Greta, for Uncle Michael, for
  our good friends Hans and Dietlinde, for parents, grandparents,
  nieces and nephews.

People worked on them for evenings on end while they listened to
  the crackling shortwave continents of *Deutsche Welle*, or
  angelic shellac gramophone records, or exquisite pages revisited
  once more, from his readings back before the war, by the man
  of the house with his spectacles propped on the bridge of his
  nose – bathed in the old, warm brown light of his desk lamp.

Easter

Like everyone else Ida prepared biscuits and drinks for Easter, she
changed clothes put on jewellery went to church – but alas,
nobody gave her a glance. It seemed that nobody even heard
her voice in the communal clamour of song and celebration.
Nobody, nobody approached with friendship approached with com-
passion her dry being preserved in poisons.

In the afternoon Saxon men and boys went out "sprinkling" in small
scurrying flocks. In high spirits, they paraded proudly through
the streets wearing costumes embroidered in black and white,
high boots, their hair combed slick, bottles of cheap perfume
in their pockets.
They entered all the houses where there were young girls and women…
At every house they'd eat biscuits and little pastries and drink
the homemade wine which had been kept for the occasion.
They didn't leave a gate untried. Only at Ida's did they fail to
open the gate.
The youngest ones strutted with an accordion taking the lead. My
friends went out in the village streets hair smartly combed,
dressed up like young men in the city. But they still returned
to their former selves when no one was looking at them from
behind curtains (or perhaps when they knew they were being
watched…). Karli would wear his suspenders that had been
embroidered with The Queen's Flower by his grandmother.
Klaus had on his outgrown trousers, oak leaves and acorns
made from coloured bits of cloth appliquéed on the tight and
short trousers, and he also wore a hat. Hermann feigned indif-
ference – 'I'm not really part of this… I couldn't care less' –
then, in a twinkling, he darted behind a gate and stole off by
himself.
They were competing to use up the biggest bottle of perfume they
could buy.
The older men, dressed up and merry, came by with some dignity.
Childlike forgetfulness, holy forgetfulness on this day unlike the
string of grey, anxious days.

But Ida's gate no one ever wanted to open.
With her arms crossed in her parched silence – a barren mountain –
Ida cursed.

At the Bus Stop, in Winter

At the first gleam of daylight, people began showing up at the cross-
roads to wait for the rural bus. By noon they were frozen to
their bones, though swaddled in their warmest clothes, with
fur collars. Wrapped in wool shawls, they stamped stiff, numb
feet beside sacks baskets cardboard suitcases tied with cords,
scuffed with age. They never grew talkative. Once in a while
someone fumbled through his baggage, seized with worry. A
few young men happened to be on their way to military service
– abstracted faces, absent eyes – they were going into the army
with a wooden footlocker handed down from father to son,
passed on from brother to brother.

At last the bus came puffing (a placard in the windscreen: 'Braşov –
Bran – Moieci – Fundata – Câmpu-Lung'), chugging and
reeking of gasoline, with thousands of smells coiling tightly
inside. There wasn't room for a pin to fall.
Two or three would get off – the others pressed against one another,
they handed children above their heads, baggage, pushed suit-
cases through legs and shoved them under seats, or up above
on the racks. Until they all climbed on, the driver stood out-
side, imperious, phlegmatic; then he turned the crank in the
pug nose of the bus to restart the engine.
Inside you could read about how to exit in case of emergency: up
through the roof.
Words and costumes mingled from the two sides of the Carpathians,
across a frontier which had been obliterated long ago and for-
gotten in the grass somewhere near Bran. A kind of fettered
hope, a lean sort of cheer with clipped wings was everyone's
portion, irrespective of their garb.

At last, slowly, the bus would creep down the slope. In its drowsy
warmth, people started gossiping.

'One thing's for sure,' Uncle Fritz joked, 'from here you can get to
Germany easier than up that hill there to Codlea.'

Evening

Every evening my grandmother would let down her blonde hair while
I watched it fall to her waist: then she braided it again. She
switched off the light. She kneeled – the whisper of her prayer
reached as far as the edges of night, fluttering His celestial gar-
ments. Her head would shine in the dark. Crouching on my bed,
I too recited my prayers, quickly, the Lord's Prayer and then,
'*Ich bin klein mein Herz ist rein…*' I prayed for everyone in the
house and also for Aunt Edith and Uncle Fritz. At the end, I tried
to persuade Him to give me hair as fairy-tale-like as Grand-
mother's ('Such foolishness,' Mama said when I confessed, 'it's
what's under the hair that counts')…the kind of hair on which
a wandering prince might climb my tower as on a ladder.
I always slept in the same room with my grandmother, and she would
become so frightened when I would sleepwalk past her in the black
dead of night. Aunt Edith explained to me that the moon rays were
summoning me when they touched my eyelids. She told me I
was 'looking for the moon', as they say in German. Only that I
was looking for which side of the earth the moon might be on.

*

Once when I was in the hospital in the city, an old, old woman slept
in the bed next to mine – they said that she was in the hospital
because at home she didn't have what she needed. They were
kind to her. They were getting ready to do surgery on her feet
in order to keep her there longer.
She had been living by herself. She didn't love children. In the daytime
she gossiped with me about every manner of trifle, 'like a lady'.
She had come from some place where there had been beauty,
riches, rivers of champagne, grand balls. About this former
world she would say hardly a word. Perhaps, like Ida, she'd
made some sort of mistake?
At night in the hospital ward, the moon would shine on her face, on
her white feet with bunions like tubers.
In my transparent sleep, it seemed to me I could distinguish her very
being in a haze, her flesh like an ethereal curtain scarcely clinging
to her bones – how it danced with stiff curving claws on her legs.

Up to the peak of the mountain of sleep, on top of the moon, she
would dance night after night.

Ţica Doaii

Ţica Doaii, an elderly peasant woman with a friendly face (a face long and dark, lit by a flame from within), foretold the future in coffee grounds.

With a neutral voice, detached from her body, she would 'read' both the good and the bad – just as she found them in the black and white maps in the cup, with thousands of faces. She would herald little joys with great indifference. Sometimes she pronounced grave verdicts. Smashed fates. Then the ladies would ask her: 'Could there not be some escape, nevertheless, despite everything, something...'

'Oh, no, no. What, do you think I should tell you lies?...' Ţica Doaii lowered her voice and lifted her burning black eyes from the hollow of the cup.

'Look, here, you'll cry many tears. Many tears. But you yourself will go on with your life. It's not really that bad. At the end, right there, this shows a brightness in the clearing. Because you'll wind up with a lighter heart.

'It's only me myself that... Whatever I do, can you see – here? How heavy my heart must be?'

Then Ţica Doaii would take another cup in her hand and lower her dark eyelashes. She kept silent for a long time.

The slanting rays from the windows divided themselves between the ladies' rings and her kerchief.

'You, Madam, you have set your thoughts on something. Your mind is always focused on another place, somebody draws it somewhere else. It starts at home, but, look, it doesn't stay there. (No, don't tell me, you mustn't tell what it is!) It's not going to turn out. But don't you grow angry, don't you brood. God Himself always knows better...'

On the Dobrice

The two brothers were the masters of the Dobrice, the road that was
a steep precipice at the far end of the Romanian Village. These
"bad boys" had crewcuts and were wondrous scamps.

Their father, a country teacher, used to tell us fairy-tale after fairy-
tale, and he sang us ballads from former worlds, most of them
sad. Afterwards, in his low kitchen, he put away the dishes –
then he arranged us in a row along one side of the table, in
order that we write from dictation…

'If you desire to show respect for yourself and your parents, for the
place where you saw the light of day,' he said, 'well then, you
have to be able to write your forefathers' tongue properly' (this
is how he always put it).

I don't know if I wanted to achieve whatever he said, but when we
made mistakes, we were very ashamed.

He started reading out the dictation – and suddenly the familiar
words seemed something else: whatever you knew looked as
if you didn't, and now you had to learn everything again.

'Nobody is born a scholar, what did you suppose?…' the teacher
consoled us – 'not even the birds in the sky, though they seem
to find it so easy to fly and twitter.

'These days, school is free,' he went on, 'for whoever happens to be
in it. These are our times. School moulds cheap gentlemen,
without requiring them to learn the least thing. It's painless,
now…but it might well become painful.

Children, you *will* learn!'

His two sons kept fidgeting mischievously on their chairs, their legs
completely covered with scratches from their play.

Ţica Doaii from the neighbourhood used to come to their house
from time to time – she mended their clothes, she helped in
the garden. 'What are you saying?! Hey, don't give me a sick
headache!' she burst out, astonished at who knows what, while
the teacher went on reading to us from a notebook and I scrut-
inised the kitchen shelves, lined with many much-thumbed
books: *The Tale of Words* and *Tom the Fool* and *The Most
Beautiful Poems Ever Written*. For years, those books had
been handed on in turn to all the neighbourhood children.

The teacher's boys were magical. Into their household, there would come as a guest Thirsty Man, who drank a dozen casks of wine to save Prince Charming, and when they aimed a stone at some little mouse they were helped by The Man Who Sees Through Things, while Bird Man enticed them to climb trees high up to the tender crown where you could touch the sky.

We listened together as their father told us about the singer-monk Anton Pann, about Şincai who had travelled with manuscripts in his old leather shepherd's wallet, about wandering, sorrowful Prince Avram, about the martyrdom of Brâncoveanu at the hands of the Turks.

He also told us about Trajan and his Dochia, about handsome princes and the peoples of forest fairies: they were attending a wedding party at the same time that we ourselves, a pack of children, went to the bakery with ration scrip clutched moist in our palms ('Did you also let Livia know that they have bread now?' 'Oh no, dearie, bless me, I forgot...').

Their mother, the two boys told me, lived in an enchanted field just over the horizon, and she had made friends with a ferret and an otter, with a wolf and a bird. And there where she stays, so sweet and kind (her face washed with mist, bracelets of fog on her wrist), is a banquet table laid out with food and drink, with lots and lots of people. And all of them surrounded by seven little windows, each with little bars in seven rows.

That is to say, exactly like in our world, right here among us – but much more luminous, with lights in the bee fields, flowers in bright meadows, green budding willows beside the Holy Mother.

In daytime she rocks for as long as she pleases between two towering fir trees. At night in her sons' dreams she draws near their bed, on a path as narrow as the finest thread.

This is how those mischievous boys, with their heads gleaming, cropped almost bald, would speak in riddles and charms from Ţica Doaii: their smile tangled in sadness, their voice floating on a teardrop.

At the Bend of the Don

At the Bend of the Don tavern, heavy shepherd's greatcoats smelling
    of sheepfolds, fur caps pushed to the backs of heads, fur caps
    on tables and on the floor
a young man with his face half burned by the sun, half white and
    delicate, passed out on the floor scrubbed black with kerosene
    – smiling in his sleep like a child
and words and shouting and brawling and crying and stories and
    laughter again / Rage without forgiveness
and new words sounded out letter by letter, flashing like new gal-
    vanised sheet metal through the thick steam of strong sweet
    wine harsh brandy raw *ţuică* the smog of cheap cigarettes,
    Zare Drojdie Rachiu Secărică Naţionale Carpaţi –

rising above, never still, the hoarse voice of the National Radio.

Rosi

Rosi tosses a small key from her window,
and the passer-by with hair in black ringlets catches it.

Rosi embroiders a tablecloth – blue flowers round and round, in the
    middle a red heart –
and the shadow of the passer-by with eyes like embers glides inside.
He's in such a hurry to come in. He's in such a hurry to go. He stays.

Refugees

The retired Colonel Broşteanu had come as a refugee from Bessarabia, and they lodged him in Ida's courtyard next to the Veterinary Clinic. He was an old man and very skinny: a coat rack on top of which dishevelled grey hair stood up like a rooster's comb. With his bluish face, his hooked nose, his sharp chin, he seemed a caricature, a silhouette cut out in jest. Early in the morning, with great solemnity, he would cross the courtyard, the chamber pot in his hand.

Mrs Colonel, his wife, would 'happen upon' my mother in some corner and tell her about their life in 'normal times'. A few minutes were enough for her to describe the villa that they'd owned, every floor covered in Persian rugs into which their footsteps sank; no doubt they also had handmade rugs on their interior staircase, too. They had been lucky to inherit fine heirlooms, no, that she couldn't complain about. Oh, the Gobelins the cheval glasses as large as a wall the crystal what splendours brought by steamship on the Danube from Vienna from Czechoslovakia – when they happened not to be French –

yes, the gilt woodwork and the loggias, the espaliered hedgerows and the arbours…what a pity, my dear, this garden of Ida's, it's merely a common village garden. 'Well, and have you been downtown today? Did they deliver any groceries to the *Alimentară*?… And so, what I was telling you about was our villa in the city. But let me describe our estate in the countryside!…'

All in one single breath. She herself seemed to have been made out of white dough, Mrs Broşteanu. Just her mouth appeared brilliantly painted on – her eyebrows pencilled in, her hair dark, dark black under her common-ration muslin kerchief. A buxom and awkward old bird: she fed on the plump, round berries of Time, as big as her desperate, round eyes.

She tried with every ounce of her being to keep the blade of the guillotine, poised above the whole landscape, from falling.

The Chest with Old Things

In the painted chest downstairs, old finery velvets ribbons silks be-
    headed from their first lives, crammed above rows of doubtful
    remembrances,
here and there a wine stain, a cigarette burn, a cotillion of perfumes.
    Waiting for – once a year – the Fancy Dress Ball. Once, once
    upon a time.

On the Way to School

I would pass the clock tower (the big hand climbing at an angle,
    climbing), then there were a couple of gates in the walls with
    their wooden shutters before I reached *him*, never absent from
    his window. Between scaly wings of weathered grey wood –
    his big shiny skull. Drool dribbling out of his slack lips.
How far beyond the window-sill he leaned out toward us, with his
    paws like stiff wet shovels, oh how he grinned, how he squealed,
    how excited he was…
Other times it happened that he kept within himself as in a shop
    window, where he alone could be in control. In his silent
    thicket, he looked forlorn.
And then his terrible fury when the boys in the street teased him
    (he had hair as boyish and bristly as on their crewcut heads).
    Or sometimes his braying and howling without any cause.
We girls would stare at him from a distance, occasionally until the
    tower clock started to sound the hour: eight o'clock, in eight
    unhurried circles. While the old clock still was pealing the
    final rings, we crossed the threshold of the classroom into the
    heavy smell of wood and diesel oil. We slipped into our seats,
    ready (the reassuring scent from the old wooden body of the
    desks with their inkwells, the sharp scent of the quill ink pens,
    the warm scent of pencils).

We kept running away from the territory of this sick boy, from the
   shadow of his house, as if – like in the old story – over our
   shoulder we threw behind us a comb from which the good
   water began to gush forth, from which
a forest, too, sprang up, and the forest swallowed the monsters and
   the miasmas, and so we could journey farther on, carefree and
   merry,
we could run around laughing in full daylight (grinning pity horror
   trickling down our faces).

We had never seen his parents.
He was ours. He was there for us. Framed in our fairy-tale every
   morning.

When we learned that his window with the grey wooden shutters
   would never again reveal him to us, we hadn't seen him for
   some time. How long?
The hands of the clock would climb toward the top of the round
   hours in the same way, like old people.
When we came near the steep sides of the church, we were sure it
   had to be the beating of a captive wing that we heard.

The Doctor

A poor peasant boy in Transylvania in the 1920s, he had been sent to
   study in Paris with the support of the community, as much as
   they could come up with. His mama would carry wood slung on
   her back, and she 'hired out' in order to be able to give her son
   some help at the École de Médecine. He and other students also
   made money singing in small bars in the Latin Quarter, and they
   played sad country airs and gay dances on the wooden flute
   the grass blade the fiddle, dressed in folk costumes from home.
He became engaged to a French girl. But her parents didn't want to
   let her go with him so far away. She was their only child: she
   had to remain in France, and he had to understand.
'I don't know whether *you* can understand,' the young man tried to
   explain. 'Here, you have everything you need.' (Between his
   words at that distant time and his words as he repeated them
   now, a curious echo, stretched and frayed.) 'In your country
   things are good. They sent me here to become a doctor for
   my poor, downtrodden peasants – whose fate we have no way
   of knowing whether it will be any better from now on.'
He returned home by himself. He'd become silent. He was continu-
   ously travelling the rural roads to tend to his patients. Long,
   narrow, winding roads. Often, though, his eyes were transfixed
   in their depths by joy – like the young, free gallop of a horse.

When at last he returned home from forced labour on the Danube
   Canal, for a very long time he kept his bags packed and ready
   – as he had learned *there*. He hadn't ever taken out the little
   cross he'd sewn into his cheap padded greatcoat. '*There* I had
   occasion to see quite a number of people who'd been brought
   back...' For years afterwards his soldier's wooden footlocker
   was ready for when they would take him again.
'You know, it was there I found I had it in myself to eat dog-meat:
   it was the Colonel's dog. My colleagues went so far as to pre-
   serve some of it. One of them was especially skilled – he was
   a doctor like me. From Iaşi.' He also told us about a young
   man from another work gang there: that boy, after having set
   his burden on his back, trudged to the scansion of Latin hex-
   ameters...to let *them* know he had not given up.

*

She came to us by herself while he was gone, especially at night, when she could get away from her work, from the children. She entered without a word, with hurry in her big, fair frame after running here on the road as if without stopping to breathe. 'Have you found out anything?' my mother would ask, always with doubt. Luci would shake her head. No.

And all at once she would break down and cry, she would sob without stopping for many slow minutes until, her face disfigured, she would raise her eyes from the floor, and she would say she'd had a dream…a dream…

he had not appeared in that dream but she felt something she sensed something it seemed to her that this…this had to be its meaning…that he…*there*…

that he had met his last end.

Frozen, Mother remained speechless. 'This cannot be, my dear friend,' Father would say softly – very softly – as if she couldn't understand his words, anyway. 'This cannot be. You're an intelligent woman, you shouldn't put any faith in dreams. He's strong. He's smart. He's a believer. He's a doctor – he will take care of himself. You'll see, he'll come home.'

'No, don't talk so lightly.' Her voice broke the silence. 'While I *haven't known a thing* about him for years. What it's like where he is…

'What can it be like there?…

'And what do they want from him, what do they want *without any trial*, for so long? They don't even care to invent reasons. What reason could there be? When he has always helped everybody …maybe that's why…because in the dead of night, when they came to find him to see some sick soul on the Dobrice, or in God knows what hole – and he never refused, no, he never refused.

'But why am I saying this, to you? As if you didn't know it too well. And you don't refuse them either. May it be your good fortune never to learn what people really deserve, as Iancu has!' She kept pouring out her words and crying. At length she would stand up, calmer. I'd been playing with my dolls in their corner, but I couldn't see them, for my eyes had become blurry.

'…Well, I came to see you when the children can't know, so they don't get scared themselves. And people shouldn't know. Because for many, however much good we did for them, now they're afraid to greet me. They see me in the street, they cross to the other side… And with others, it's worse – when they arrive at my door smiling and act smothering to me, without any cause. With so much sympathy that I can't tell what's what…'

*

Children never talk about as much as they understand. Children look around without asking whether their neighbour went to work in the morning, or maybe he was *taken* last night and nobody knows anything about him, maybe only his wife, who could see him in dreams. Sometimes, once in a while, she might hear word of him, from strange travellers.

Children never talked about that. They didn't mention anything about how they were listening to hope / anxiety. Human teeth grinding on chains.

...I'd been hearing for some time how Comrade Stalin was ill. His fever climbed higher: every day he was worse. The radio voice sounded lugubrious. And then the blackest moment arrived, when 'The Dear Father' died, and the radio voice trembled like a big earthquake in the air.

I understood that from now on we were a species of orphans – That One had perished who'd given us life. (I was crying and nobody had the courage to stop me.)

My house was filled with joy 'That One's dead... God knows,' they whispered, 'it's impossible not to see changes now.'

Nevertheless years passed before the doctor, my godfather, came home from *there*. Justice happens without hurry.

There was simply a time I somehow knew: *he'd come*. On the following day I heard his slow, heavy steps in our courtyard. His shadow gliding across the windows.

He entered the house. I couldn't look at him at first. He seemed to me ...as heavy as the earth. The light billowed in waves (...'What a big, strong girl you've become. Oh, and do you know how to read?'...). He had a gravelly voice. He started rolling a cigarette.

With his firm step and his shiny, round leather physician's bag full of instruments, as heavy as the earth indeed – in stature, he was short, and thin, and as before he had to go long years and many winding roads to tend to sick people.

He built a house for his family, he installed the electrical and the gas connections with his own hands. He worked a lot so as to provide everything they would need.

And then, before his time, he departed from among us.

The Metamorphosis

While the war was sweeping from frontier to frontier, and columns of soldiers on their way to the front marched by singing, the women the young girls the children waited for them in groups at crossroads and accompanied them with tears in their eyes for quite some distance until they watched them disappear slowly over the horizon. But it isn't good to follow someone with your eyes until he's lost from the light: they say you'll never see that person again.

During that time when these things were unfolding, and experienced, shrewd farmers portioned out their fodder and the food in storage with the utmost care, Heini attended teacher training school. He was a diligent student. He never left for tomorrow what he could do today. If he had a little spare time, he made use of it to play the violin and the accordion. He was the best student in his school. His elderly host family, in the city, loved him dearly. Sundays, Heini would go mountain-climbing.

On his vacations he could see Lotte, at long last. The young girl who was to become his bride. The most beautiful young girl in Transylvania, everyone said. He missed her every hour of the day. She had been given by God to one of the smallest houses, to the poorest of parents, ignorant and withered. But she was the pride of the neighbourhood. And Heini was the proudest of all the young boys, because he would have her for his wife.

The Fates give, the Fates take away, as it pleases them. Heini had just become engaged to Lotte when, right after the war, the young girl was transported to Russia. To the mines. And there was hunger, and there was cold: she could see death with her own eyes every minute, as in an accursed mirror. With those shades yet drawing breath, she shared the dish of one who had died by her side, frozen – and they managed to get him counted for one more day, through negligence. And maybe another.

When Lotte came back, you couldn't recognise her any longer. Her
    eyes had sunk deep in their sockets, crossed. Her jaw protruded.
    Her back was permanently bent. Her hair looked colourless
    and straggly. When she tried to laugh, her voice crumbled
    like sawdust. Her mind lost itself in a wispy fog.
Heini had waited for her desperately. Immediately he married her.
    He played the violin and the accordion for days on end.
In time the memory of the beautiful face of his bride faded, became
    erased.
He didn't know why they'd been chosen for punishment.
He didn't know how to pay the ransom to whatever wizard.
Nor did it ever happen that his wife turned three somersaults at mid-
    night and on the spot transformed into a beautiful princess
    until the earliest light of dawn.
Together they lived the death of their time and their place, drop by
    drop by drop. With their face averted from the reflection of
    any meaning.

Their daughter, though, had long red hair, she was clever, and her
    proud and beautiful bearing revealed ancient folk memories
    from the Rhine.

Summer Afternoon

From the heart of the mountains the gypsies would descend with
    wild strawberries blueberries raspberries in deep, narrow
    wooden pails balanced on ropes over their shoulders.
They would tell you tales of how a bear chased them how a snake
    almost bit them how they had almost been swallowed forever
    by the precipice.
Their fingers – gleaming ebony from the picking from the juices
    from the earth – would uncover the treasure. The cool red
    flames bared themselves between soft fangs of fern.

Placed in broad porcelain bowls, the fruit would raise high its
    untamed scent – a sword.

Landscape

Raven-black hair spreading wide in the air. An ample, cherry-red mouth. Eyebrows and eyelashes like fine combs. Her nails long and red, sparkling. She moved among everyone else noisy and jittery. A mask.

A courtly gentleman, expert in crosswords. He used to smoke thin cigarettes. People liked to have him around for his conversation. He had big eyes. He looked deeply. His mind was anywhere but here. His each word, precisely calculated.

Another gentleman, he would only glance sidelong. But he could see through the walls. His questions aimed at very precise targets. His smile: a slice through the air, though it had little to do with him personally.

The priest's wife dwelled in never-failing frivolity. And falsehood. But for this the priest didn't cut off her tongue. She'd offer up lies even when nobody asked her anything. She was aflutter in colours and glitter in order to camouflage herself. Her words would tumble into their slots without mistake. The laughter on her cheeks of crumpled cardboard.

People used to laugh a great deal in those days, wearing everyday faces.

Some of them inhabited a narrow place. Others swelled to the horizon. People with pale blue-grey walls, stairways rotting inside (their faint smiles crooked and tight).

People who had come from beyond the Prut, from beyond the Danube, from no one knows where. Whom the times had flung into this angle of the Carpathians. It was quiet, the quiet of wariness. And something more, a slow poisoning. Droplets of poison of an indeterminate toxicity.

Every now and again individuals cut across the street obliquely, cap pushed down over their foreheads: the bearers of edicts. They had no faces. Nobody succeeded in catching their glance. But you could feel the burning of their eyes on your skin. They'd steal back across the street obliquely when they departed.

: By the very next day, undercover, yet another neighbour had been
     picked up.
And on the following day the drummer summoned the people to the
     crossroads. He announced the government's will. Everybody
     assembled in a hurry. Then they returned home – silent, dim-
     inished.

'…As far as where?… What! What kind of law is that?' an old man
     found himself exclaiming loudly. He stood motionless, leaning
     on his cane with the entire burden. His eyes, as large as his face,
     were extinguished gradually. They hadn't heard him. Only some
     children remained there with him.

The Priest

The priest would speak and sing unintelligibly – nothing in his face
     stirred. I'd been warned he would cut off my tongue any time
     I blurted out something not proper or told a lie. I followed his
     big eyes, half closed under the thick lids. When he came near,
     I was afraid. The smoke from the censer sliced into my breath.
People were whispering to one another, very close. As I passed, my
     nose got stuck in their clothes pungent from moth flakes. What
     people were saying was that the priest quarrels with the other
     priest, and shoves him even in the holy altar ('For shame, for
     shame, at their age, God forbid! They should know better!').
     People grumbled to one another – but suddenly they fell within
     themselves, each immersed in private concerns and unspoken
     worries. An invisible heart touched their suffering.
In a moment their faces became cleaner, placid. From their depths,
     they raised their eyes to the vault pierced by shafts of light
     and they crossed themselves. At the end they kissed the icon
     placed on the long embroidered cloth ('A GIFT OF LIVIU AND
     CORNELIA POP for the souls of all in their household') and
     they received the myrrh on their forehead.

The Brick Kiln

We went on this excursion through the woods only once, the whole
school. We felt it was an adventure, we imagined we were a
multitude, 'grown-ups', free. On the path broken by roots and
the jagged edges of stones, we hiked along, singing. Herr Liess
('Comrade Teacher') would hum some opening bars – like a
riddle – and we'd be ready, we'd start to sing about geese and
foxes, about migrating birds, about the miller's wanderlust or
Hänschen who set out into the wide, wide world, about jolly
hunters, the dearest of letters from far away, the wedding feast
tomorrow, sweet-sad longing today.

When we halted, our noise would seep down into the earth during
timeless, silent seconds. Then the stillness of the mountain
enveloped us, measureless, its imperative to listen. Like arrows
from hidden places, tiny sounds arose like millions of pins.

Some time before this, Herr Liess had told us about Kriemhild, Brun-
hild and the Nibelungs. Here, it had to have been in just this
spot, in this forest, that all those things took place. On that
day, we even found the place where Siegfried was immersed
in the river. The very oak from which the traitorous leaf had
fallen upon his shoulder.

Beings were calling one another from the distance, calling. A bell
open in the silence, our hearts responded.

In a beautiful valley with the earth torn to the bone we stopped – at
a kiln for making bricks. Through a window looking inward
toward the bowels of the earth, we could see a ball of domes-
ticated fire. The brick maker, a German as ancient as the earth
itself, lived nearby. Among his moulds and bricks he was the
loneliest of men. But he was the one who knew when the bricks
were ripe, from two iron stalks heated red in the big, gentle fire.

There we learned that houses grow from the bowels of the earth –
and that first they had to be immersed in fire to the smallest
essential.

And that before arriving at the old brick maker's hut, at his kilns,
you had to cross the river where Siegfried paused to drink,
hot with hunting – there where they had bathed him, on that
very first day – and a leaf had fallen upon his shoulder.

Black Bread

black bread with lard
when we swore our oaths one for all
all for one

black bread and three lumps of sugar
work first – play after

black bread with bacon
may tattletales and double-crossers die

Discipline

The blood throbs in your sight in your hearing red black red black
    the blood throbs
when you cannot raise your eyes to anyone
and if you raised them, you could not see –
when you've made a mistake
when a vagabond word got snagged on your tongue, and that's enough
    for all of them, laughing uproariously, to understand where
    you've been

when everything had been following along in a humdrum row of days,
    one and the same – then suddenly, *no!*
you're by yourself, isolated, with your bridges drawn up. Their glances
    strike directly at you –
or maybe His watchful gaze only, Whom you cannot see through
    the rays of light.

The blood throbs in your sight in your hearing, blinding you, you
    cannot distinguish joy, pain,
alone within yourself in the flame you no longer can distinguish
    anything.

And you have only to learn (while the beast goes on gnawing at
    your body) to smile as if nothing's happened: suspended in a
    mute prayer, patiently counting to yourself, above the Void

until in the end the river-bed faithfully reclaims its waters.

In the Street Outside the Grocery

On a little table in the street outside the door to the *Alimentară*,
    they were selling cornmeal, packaged neatly in small bags
    folded into a point: but only two kilograms per person. The
    line was three abreast and very long.
A man stood nervously, a man not from the village, a man like a
    mountain (could he have been a shepherd?). He knew nobody,
    not a soul from his own village whom he might exchange a
    word with.
When he finally made it to the table, he paid politely, but then he
    lifted the cornmeal in one of his huge hands. He took a stride
    backwards and, in front of everybody, he straightened up and
    towered into the air as big as he could be, he gathered himself
    up to hurl the package to the cobblestones:
'Who are they giving this paper sack of nothing to? Who, to us? Is
    this supposed to be enough to cook ourselves *mămăligă* and
    also feed our livestock?…
'May the earth swallow these gangsters!'

The cornmeal spread in the mud like a famished, living tongue.

Airy Structures

Airy structures glide on pulleys, in transformation –
walls arch over lives ever more alien.

Here and there a god crouches elbows on knees on the lintel spanning
    a gate
a little transparent god who must serve many houses for some time
    to come.

Healing

All alone, isolated in the dark rooms, Ida's inner being steeped in
venom through and through – an overripe fruit ready to plummet
through air itself venomous. All alone in her rooms – while
life constantly hurried past her doorstep, wave after wave.

But one day she left the door open. One day it was sunny.

That day a little boy climbed up to Ida's threshold. He was so blond
you'd almost have to say he had threads of light on his tousled
head. Ida stood astonished. The boy looked her straight in the
eye, his glittering dark eyes round with joy. Suddenly his joy
grew greater, leapt into his whole body, and, quickly, expertly,
he started crawling toward her. This was the son of the people
next door, whom she hated.

She took the child in her arms. Furtively. 'What's that?' he asked
right away in his own way of speaking. 'What's that?' In the
darkened rooms you could see the glint of silverware, heavy
bronze cups, curtains embroidered with gold thread – in the
child's eyes thousands of stars must have exploded. Ida lifted
the boy in her arms to show him. 'What's that?' She offered
him dry, stale biscuits from a tray.

In the end, he kissed her parched cheek with a sticky mouth full of
biscuit crumbs.

'Will you come here again?' she asked. (A strange hope had invad-
ed her being. Under the stiff folds of her clothing, she seemed
to breathe more freely.) The child answered *yes*, with his chin
hard against his chest – twice, in the style of a man: *yes, yes.*

*

This was God's will with Ida: it was my infant brother who softened
her. Soon all of us dared to come near her. She had become
very kind and good to us. She could laugh happily. We spent
a lot to time with her.

When we had colds as children and felt burning hot with fever,
instead of injections and drugs, Ida would wrap us in wet
sheets and cover us warmly, she would sing to us – and in the
morning we were better.

She told us lots of stories from the time she was a child in the Prater, in Vienna. And one time when she was on a vacation train I don't remember where in the mountains, she said that you would have thought the train was about to shake into pieces from the great speed, that's how much it clattered and banged, and the ladies' hair kept blowing loose from under their hats. But if you were to look objectively – a horse could have carried you just as fast!

(How grey now, how small she had become in her clean dress of inexpensive linen.)

She also told us about such a great flood in our Rose Valley that part of her father's house, big and solid like a boyar's, was torn away. When the churning and the roaring had abated, men went out following the path of the water, downstream along the Bârsa. They tried to collect what things they might find and bring them to the church. 'Whose wonderful blouse is this?' asked the priest admiring the exquisite lace. 'It's mine.' Ida recognised it – with great pride. She had embroidered it herself – the gown meant to be her bridal gown. The waters had ripped it in two. Of all that had been washed away by the flood, this was the only thing they could find.

She confessed to my mother, only to her, how much she had hated us. 'Who knows why? In the end God willed that my soul be freed from that curse. (We're sure to be the merest playthings of our hearts...the old priest who died kept trying to teach us that. The new one we have now is too young to know what's what!) I was boiling with hatred like a pot in hell, maddened with so much simmering passion. Evening after evening I'd overhear your radio through the door between... I could sometimes understand things, when the announcers' voices broke free of the interference and static. Radio Free Europe, Voice of America – how easy it would have been for me to do evil!... God forbid! At the time it was a sickness – but – even then, there was a point I wouldn't go beyond.

'And I never had guests, so fortunately there was no one else to hear...'

Then?... And then?

In the end Ida sewed some fancy sheets with scalloped edges, for us to keep for many years.

Soon after that, we departed from the village.

Surrounded at last by some distant cousins from her own family,
who finally were permitted to live with her there, in her house
which had been designed for another kind of life,
she, too, soon departed...as light as a dandelion puffball, she departed.

At the Old Fortress

Looked at from high above in the old fortress, life down in the court-
yards and garden plots flickered like a tiny flame. Dreamy lanes
crawled out into the fields like millipedes.
Throughout the rooms deep inside the circular ruins, harmless weeds
grew, sweet grass, while the baneful leaves of nettle reached
skyward. Here and there trees clung to the stone slabs with
powerful claws sucking life from the walls; their leaves rustled
in the drowsy air.

We measured our breath and voices against the high crown of the
castellated walls, free as far as the shoulders of the mountains
as far as the imperial flight of the eagle. There was peace,
vertical peace, all around the old fortress. And space for life,
sweetness.
Each time, we would measure our own being against the battlements
of the old fortress – our promised being which we would forget
about afterwards, day after day.
With their shrill shrieks birds wheeled round and round intimating
fortresses in the air: their flight, an immeasurable thirst.

We were coming by sledge from the heart of the mountain down to
where it lost itself and flattened into the fields.
Our souls – hot fiery earth – in disintegration. The instant in dis-
integration like a star. The self would descend from the kernel
of fire to the diminished, shallow day – under the day's half-
shut eyelids.

The First Warning

What did that day mean, what did it want from me, that first day so
    deafening but soundless? I kept my silence, uncomprehending,
    very far from silent knowledge / until then, unquestioning of
    everything.

A bodiless arrow, the light set forth to seek out my Solitude. My
    breath found itself pinned to the distant edges of the world,
    affixed with pine needles.

What did that day require? The earth diffused its scent from its secret
    belly. The mountains, warmed, had begun melting.
The air commenced on its great journey. It gazed at me from close by.
    From very close. From no distance at all.

In my stasis, I could feel time's pain, as if under anaesthesia.

The Bârsa Land

The Bârsa Land, flat ocean of wheat and poppies extending as far
    as the foot of the mountains,
carts laden with light rays, processions, portals – a landscape cease-
    lessly flowing high above the clusters of wise roofs, with two
    or three twinned steeples: villages sheltered in gussets where
    the mountain tucks itself beneath the plain.
Shrines and wellheads from various peoples. Solitary crosses where
    somebody or other happened to have died – a child or grown-
    up – struck by lightning on the very spot, near the cattle or at
    harvest.
Creeks without bridges where we crossed carefully. We halted in
    the current of icy water, and after the horse had drunk its fill,
    when it would have liked to throw us into the stream and be
    free to swim, Father pulled back on the reins and we started
    off again.

The sun flicked our faces softly with long switches of light. The
    hooves beat unhurriedly on the asphalt road. Everywhere on
    earth, you could see the light at play in vertical shafts.
Sometimes on hot days rain would also fall, in straight creases, from
    big blinding eyes in the sky; and the rain cut across our way,
    more luminous than light itself, as if a game with masks.

Between factories, the Bârsa wended its way, flowing ever thicker
    with chemicals.

At Home

Aunt Edith opens the old cookbook with the coat of arms stamped
    in gold on the black cover. She breaks five eggs into a bowl,
    weighs the exact amount of sugar on the scales, then flour.
    Taking the butter from its paper, she scrapes the wrapper with
    a Rostfrei knife (on its handle 𝕰𝕳 – her monogram surrounded
    by delicate tendrils of holiday Gothic).
Aunt Edith takes a long, long time ironing the sheets with their lace
    and embroidery of the family coat of arms combined with the
    diadem and roots of Braşov, City of the Crown.

In the half-open drawers of the desk, Faber Castell pencils Hardmuth
    pencils, still left from other times, release their scent.
It was turning darker.
Under Turner's mists, on the calendar, Uncle Fritz repastes the days
    into next year using the days from the year gone by.

I Know How to Speak

I know how to speak
as if I'm not speaking
I know how to speak without moving my lips
my face motionless
I know how to speak so you
can't detect who and when

– as if the wind had uttered
my words

The Man

Sometimes when we were just by ourselves, Aunt Edith and me, I'd ask her as sweetly as I could, oh, please, oh, please, take the encyclopaedia down from the shelf (the row of heavy volumes covered in gold on leather with delicate scents from long ago) – the book where The Man lived.

From this man you could undress layer after layer: like the altar doors we called king's gates, first the skin was removed from the muscles on the left side and then on the right.

Red fibres like fins could be raised off the bones; they trembled from our quiet breathing. When you next opened the transparent sheet drawn like a diaphanous jewel, you came to the marrow where juices rose like the earthy liquors in trees, in plant stalks. From under the ribs looking like prison bars the lungs emerged like large insect wings, and inside the lungs branches grew, heavy with blossoms.

The heart seemed tilted, a pretty, coloured little house with tiny rooms and doors out of which blue and red roads multiplied to the faraway reaches of their territory in crazy torrents of liberty, sniffing after the boundary markings of their range – numberless fingers intertwined, an every-second clutching of death with life, the drop of new blood from the thick poison of the old blood.

Intricate streets reservoirs faces of leaves so many interior maps, the secret of secrets in the colours of mother-of-pearl and rose and ivory.

The Man was a man and The Man was a woman. It was all of us at once.

Farther and farther – the silky walls of every organ, ribs muscles clasping round and embracing the whole work.

Even in the crystal-clear eye a lot of hiding places could be revealed. The wizard eye of the visible world. The eye in its swaddling as in a cradle.

The Man was glorious from head to toe – Magic: the walls thrown open to the many facets of its physical creation / half in flight half in chains.

Both of us stayed silent for a long time. I stopped breathing in order to understand. ('Doesn't it hurt him?' 'No.') Nevertheless I sensed an indelible pain threading through his whole being. I went on opening other paths among wings. In profile the head remained serene intangible aloof.

'OK, now, time to get busy,' said Aunt Edith. 'We've got to put him back as he was.' With her nearly translucent hands, covered with freckles, she folded back membrane after membrane cheek over cheek – with utmost care so as not to mix any of the many interior faces: each one according to its kind and again in its rightful niche. Exactly as they lie in my body and in yours. Organ after organ lay down to sleep in its place, still breathing the vast generous air.

Emigration

Since they've departed from the house, every last one of them – in
    the deserted household, the ancestors now gather like a braid of
    water of shadow, in empty spaces as lofty as domed centuries.
    Back to the oldest and most remote of them – they who had
    come to serve as sentries at the farthest edges of Europe, on
    horseback in carts in wagons, pleased with the peace they found
    pleased with the rich soil.
They who in the most obscure angle of the Carpathians proudly raised
    in Braşov a magnificent Black Church.

The air is heavy with remembrances as if its volume were of earth.
    The wooden frame gives a sign from the foundations. Bats
    unfurl themselves from sleep, from their velvets. As though
    issuing from the nothing of an ancient bell, a humming emerges,
    round as a child in the womb.
On this night the angel of the house comes down among them: out
    from the door of the hay attic, launching into motion with a
    single beat of the wings. Wrinkled robes, one long straw cling-
    ing to the hem. A loose sheet from a child's ABC fluttering,
    fluttering.

Before the Journey all of them gather for the last time (oh, the aroma
    of lily and vanilla…below, in the cellar, a door bangs by itself).

They are together, all of them under the roof which – after tomorrow
    – will give shelter to others:

Blessed be this house once more which now becomes disentangled
    from our ways.
O Lord, grant us this day a sign of recognition.

When I Departed

With His arm, He had made a circumference around the children's
sweet-diseased world: they sat at the edge of that kingdom.
Prepared to depart. A tear, migratory, huge, descended as a
guide – a lens fit for several lives thereafter.

Then the long abandoned well resounded with the last stone thrown
down.
We summoned forth the last echo at the wall of the old fortress.
We still tasted the leaves of sorrel, one last petal.
We measured our being, the tallest and freest, against the high crown
of the castellated wall.
We came by sledge from the heart of the mountain down to where
it lost itself and flattened into the fields.

Yes, and we were put to rock in our cradles under the barn roof –
once again, with our bodies as shuttles, we wove a swatch of
sky above a swatch of earth worn smooth by play.
And of course we hid: shadow after shadow, the game's counting
off left us fully visible in the light – with a forced smile on
our face.

Aunt Edith baked me a pie: but no longer could I hold the mixing
bowl to help her with the crust. So I ate, ate in farewell, so as
to remember with body, with soul.

Sweet-diseased summer, autumn, young winter – oh, we were shed-
ding like leaves everything that was no longer our own. Totally
naked suspended in the moment.
From above the circles of the resounding world, slowly He withdrew
his arm.

NOTES

For readers who might want additional information about the Germans of Transylvania, who are so important to the background of the poems that make up this book, we asked historian Ernest H. Latham, Jr., to provide a brief history. We thank him for his contribution, which appears directly below, preceding the notes to individual poems.

The Transylvanian Saxons: German colonists first appeared in the region in 1143 when King Geza II of Hungary invited them into Transylvania to garrison the passes of the Carpathian Mountains against the Tartars. The settlers held back the invaders and proved equally effective against the Turks who in subsequent centuries replaced the Tartars as a threat. Although called Saxons (in Romanian, Saşi), most were not from Saxony but from the left bank of the Rhine River, largely the Rhineland, Flanders, and Mosel areas.

As the Turkish threat receded, starting in the 17th century, the descendants of the early colonists moved out from the fortified churches of the peasant villages and became important contributors to the economic life of the region as merchants and skilled craftsmen in the major cities of Transylvania, which in German became known as Siebenbürgen, 'the seven fortresses'. These walled cities developed into the important Transylvanian urban centres, known today as the Romanian cities of Braşov, Cluj, Sibiu, Sebeş, Sighişoara, Mediaş and Bistriţa (or, in their traditional German names, Kronstadt, Klausenburg, Hermannstadt, Mühlbach, Schässburg, Mediasch and Bistritz).

Despite their integration within the economy, the Saxon Germans remained culturally unassimilated, retaining their customs, folk arts, religion (which became Lutheran after the Reformation), and unique dialect of German. Although most Saxons never set foot in a German-speaking country outside of Transylvania, doctors, lawyers, clergy, and teachers attended German-language universities to the west, and thus the community's leaders reinforced each generation's ties to German culture and identity.

At the end of the First World War, with the reunification of Transylvania with Romania, the Saxon population stood at about 240,000. However, their role in the economy and society as skilled craftsmen and manufacturers, as well as their efficiency and success as farmers and tradesmen, gave the Saxons an importance beyond their numbers.

Although the Transylvanian Germans tended to concern themselves only with their small, cohesive community, some identified with the Nazi movement and supported Hitler during the Second World War. For this, the entire Saxon population paid a terrible price. In the winter of 1944-45, the Soviet army, by then virtually occupying Romania, took advantage of widespread anti-German sentiment to impose a brutal relocation programme. Thousands of men and women were deported eastwards into the Soviet Union in unheated trains with minimal provisions; large numbers perished on the way, and many others disappeared into labour camps.

The Transylvanian Saxons never recovered from the Second World War and its aftermath, including the collectivization of most of the nation's agriculture. Later, under Nicolae Ceauşescu, the Socialist Republic's tolerance of their emigration, plus the lack of human rights and severe deprivations in Romania, led to the almost total disappearance of the community. In Romania's national census of 1992, the year that *The Triumph of the Water Witch* was published in Bucharest, only 1843 citizens identified themselves as Saxons.

*   *   *

At the Beginning *(page 19)*: Behind the phrase 'the waters will turn cooler' is an old pagan belief retained in the Transylvanian Carpathians, marking the passage of the season to autumn – the Transfiguration is observed on August 6 in the Eastern Orthodox calendar. In early August, the legendary figure of the Stag (an analogue to Christ) is thought to have urinated in the rivers. After this, no one was supposed to bathe in the rivers anymore that year.

That Winter *(page 20)*: St John's Day – January 7 in the Orthodox calendar – is the day of honour for John the Baptist. *Mămăligă*, a boiled mixture of ground corn and water (like polenta or the American South's cornmeal mush), is an inexpensive staple for many Romanians, particularly in the countryside.

The Bârsa Land *(pages 23 and 82)*: The Bârsa plain or depression, a broad high valley at the south-eastern corner of Transylvania, lies within the arc of the Carpathians north of Romania's capital, Bucharest. As the mountains curve from their east-west range (the Transylvanian Alps) and turn sharply north and then north-west toward Ukraine and the Slovak Republic, they form the "angle" or "extremity" of the Carpathians that the poems speak of, protected by its peaks as if by fortifications or battlements. To natives of the Transylvanian basin, the elevated lands within the Carpathians are composed of smaller regions, defined by mountains and rivers. The Bârsa Land of the poem, crossed by the Bârsa River flowing north into the Olt River, contains rich farmland and a cluster of towns and little villages (including Râşnov, where Ieronim grew up, and also, mentioned elsewhere in the poems, Bran, Moieci and Fundata), as well as the city of Braşov. The push for industrialisation by the communist government aimed at building factories in every area of

Romania, and such rivers, even relatively isolated in the mountains, often became heavily polluted, to which the second, later poem by this title makes explicit reference.

The Triumph of the Water Witch *(page 24)*: As is noted in the Introduction, the Water Witch, among other things, explicitly evokes a recognisable post-Second World War social icon for Romanians, the Russian woman of the occupation. Romanians marvelled at the large-size watches worn by the Soviet women soldiers and apparatchiks, even small clocks strapped to their arms – and by the men, too. Hence the Water Witch is an immediately recognisable allegorical stand-in for communist control itself, while conjuring up ancient, contrasting mythic and folkloric figures of fertility and the earth's cycles.

Partisans *(page 26)*: After the Second World War, resistance to communism continued in the mountains as late as the end of the 1950s. Some of the partisans were never caught. In the Bârsa region, there was considerable long-standing resistance. The Voice of America and Radio Free Europe urged continuation of this resistance, a message heard by many despite jamming, and planes dropped propaganda material to encourage the population. It is well-known now that the Allies never intended to intervene militarily. Listening to VOA, RFE or other Western broadcasts could result in imprisonment. The whisper that the Americans were coming was a continuous refrain for almost two decades after the war.

At the Pharmacy *(page 28)*: This set of portraits of the four father figures of the communist movement, Marx, Engels, Lenin and Stalin, could be seen everywhere, and always in this, the proper order. Slowly they disappeared as the political winds changed; by the 1980s only the official portrait of Romania's dictator, Nicolae Ceauşescu, could be found.

Christmas *(page 29)*: Hess chocolates, produced in Braşov, were well known among the Saxons in Transylvania; the brand name is short for Hessheimer. In fact, the owner was the first husband of the Aunt Edith who appears later in these poems, thus her monogram '𝕰𝕳' in the poem **At Home** *(page 83)*.

Epiphany *(page 32)*: In the Eastern Orthodox tradition, Epiphany, January 6, is celebrated at the edge of a body of water, a river, the sea, a lake. It's a colourful community event, with flags or banners getting dipped in the water. The Dâmboviţa River flows south out of the Carpathians past Rucăr, where Ieronim's maternal grandmother was born, east of Câmpu-Lung (now written as one word), and through the Wallachian plain stretching from the Carpathians to the Danube (the river continues through Bucharest to join the Argeş and meet the Danube farther south). Wallachia, one of the three principalities which were united in 1918 to form modern Romania (with Transylvania and Moldavia, the latter of which had formed a union with Wallachia in 1859), historically has been defined by the mountains in the pass between Bran and Rucăr. Rucăr, along with Câmpulung, is Wallachian.

The Crown *(page 33)*: All the Transylvanian cities had multiple names, some likewise having Hungarian-language names because of a large ethnic Magyar or Székely (also called Szekler) population. Braşov/ Kronstadt became Stalin City under the Soviet occupation. In 1956, with Khrushchev's accusations against Stalin and the de-Stalinisation campaign, the name changed back; statues of Stalin were pulled down overnight.

Friends in Need *(page 36)*: On 11 June 1948, the communist government of Romania nationalised all the principal industries; owners kept their house or apartment if they had only one, but if they owned more than one residence, all were confiscated. Many owners were resettled in poverty in unfamiliar places, if not taken to the prison gulag. Agrarian expropriation and redistribution had begun earlier, with the land reform of 22 March 1945, and continued in a series of steps with the collectivization of agriculture announced in March 1949.

The Century Was Breaking in Half *(page 44)*: The one National Radio station played propaganda in public offices, factories, workplaces, restaurants, bars, etc., through single-station receivers equipped with crude, harsh loudspeakers.

Arranging the Wardrobe *(page 47)*: Capşa and Zamfirescu are pre-war, pre-communist brands of chocolate famous in Romania, Suchard an imported Swiss equivalent. The phrase 'any eventuality' is a veiled reference to the risk of sudden imprisonment or deportation into exile that persons of certain social categories – for instance, professionals, the clergy, former owners and landlords, the bourgeoisie – knew was always close by. Many prepared a stock of items, such as heavy woollen socks otherwise not needed except in the cold of unheated cells or domiciles, and some routinely kept a packed suitcase ready.

The 'Armistice' refers to events starting on 23 August 1944 when King Michael I staged a royal coup, threw out the military dictatorship of Marshall Ion Antonescu and removed Romania from the Axis powers. Romania soon declared war on Nazi Germany and joined the Allies, but only three weeks later, on 12 September, a convention of armistice with the Soviet Union (acting on behalf of the Allied Powers) amounted to an unconditional surrender to the USSR, so the 'Armistice' came to be a sarcastic euphemism for the beginning of enforced Sovietization.

Mother's Crying *(page 49)*: The litany of place-names is a recitation of important political prisons in Romania. Jilava prison, in Bucharest, was also handy for protesters at the time of the December 1989 revolution that overthrew Ceauşescu and later for ex-communist officials. Piteşti was notorious for cruel torture and 're-education'; Sighet was where the highest political class of pre-communist leaders was taken and executed. Baia Sprie was a mine for non-ferrous metals where prisoners were forced to work amid radioactive rock, among other dangers. Both Făgăraş and Gherla are centuries-old fortresses; the latter became proverbial, and the phrase 'you'll be taken to Gherla' signified a warning to be cautious or risk incarceration or some other bad fate. Aiud and Călăraşi round out this list of the harshest of political prisons in the country. Besides imprisonment, among the most humiliating punishments was harvesting reeds in the Danube Delta, where a large proportion of prisoners died.

The Ball *(page 50)*: The Ball is part of the pre-Lenten carnival season of *Fasching*, which the Transylvanian Germans celebrated.

Aunt Edith and Uncle Fritz *(page 52)*: The Râşnov Fortress was built in the 13th century by the community for protection against invasions and raids. Typically, in many Transylvanian towns, this was a circular stone edifice, a kind of fortified church, into which residents and livestock could retreat so as to withstand sieges. Such fortresses were usually built inside the towns. The one at Râşnov is on top of the nearest mountain and has only a small chapel. Its well, which appears later in the book and has run dry, was dug deep down through the entire mountain.

Holidays *(page 56)*: *Deutsche Welle* was the West German, German-language equivalent of the American Voice of America, Radio Free Europe, and the BBC World Service, all broadcasting behind the Iron Curtain.

On the Dobrice *(page 61)*: This poem is filled with specifically Romanian references from fairy-tales, literature, history and folklore.

Thirsty Man (who could drink any quantity), The Man Who Sees Through Things (a kind of cyclops with x-ray vision), and Bird Man (who catches and eats birds but can also change shape and stretch to the moon and beyond, rather like Plastic Man out of comic-book history or anthropomorphic Silly Putty), are all characters in *The Tale of Harap Alb* (alternatively, *The Tale of the White Slave*) by the 19th-century story-teller, Ion Creangă (1837-89). Creangă was a creator of tales and a reteller of peasant folklore as well as a satirist, a sort of combination of Hans Christian Andersen, the Brothers Grimm, and Mark Twain. In *Harap Alb*, the main character, a prince who is tricked into being a servant or slave to a devilish, unnatural (hairless) creature in the form of a man, is helped in his trials by these, and other, marvellous monsters, as well as benevolent fairies and figures who suggest Christian typology. The hairless man of *Harap Alb* is suggested earlier by the 'beardless youth' in the poem, **At the Pharmacy** *(page 28)*

Anton Pann and Gheorghe Şincai were important early writers in the Romanian tongue. Pann (1796-1854) was a church cantor, a musician and an expert in proverbs. Şincai (1754-1816) was a founder of the Transylvanian School, a movement fostering Enlightenment scholarship. A historian and philologist, Şincai demonstrated that the Romanian language was of Latin origin and opposed the Romanians' conditions of servitude under the Austrian empire,which controlled Transylvania; thus he was persecuted and had to carry all his material around with him in a shepherd's bag.

The Roman Emperor Trajan (who ruled 98-117) was responsible for the conquest of Dacia in 106. Dochia, a name associated with the Geto-Dacians, is a symbol of the country itself in many legends and charms. In one set of stories, she is the daughter of Decebal, the Dacian ruler who committed suicide rather than fall captive to the Roman forces; Trajan pursued her until she was transformed into a rock by the Dacian god Zalmoxis.

Avram Iancu (1824-72), a leader of the 1848 revolution against both Hungary and Austria, was called 'Prince' by the peasants as an honour. Constantine Brâncoveanu, a Prince of Wallachia who reigned 1688-1714, is culturally very important for fostering a characteristic architecture synthesising French and Italian elements as part of a Renaissance style in Romania; politically he tried to balance the principality's connections among the Ottoman Empire, which still held Wallachia in vassalage, the Hapsburgs, and Imperial Russia. He was beheaded in Istanbul by the Turks, first being forced to witness the executions of his four sons.

The animals (ferret, otter, wolf, bird) derive from a popular Romanian lament for the dead. Many villages all over Romania still symbolically conduct the dead across streams and into meadows and the fir tree forest with chants and songs; in some villages, animal masks stand for these animal companions.

At the Bend of the Don *(page 63)*: During the Second World War, in the autumn of 1942, Romanian infantry suffered huge losses fighting the Soviets on the Don when the Germans never arrived to reinforce them (their troops remained engaged at Stalingrad). The tavern's popular nickname implies a memorial not just to heroism and sacrifice but also to opposition to the Russians, although a more overt association is that it is a place of fights and arguments. Romanian home-distilled plum brandy, *ţuică* can be very harsh in its commercial forms, and Zare, Drojdie, Rachiu and Secărică are brands of cheap drink; both Naţionale and Carpaţi are cigarettes.

Refugees *(page 64)*: Bessarabia, a former territory of Romania located across the Prut River that now forms Romania's north-east border, became part of the Soviet Union in 1940 after it was effectively ceded to the

Soviets in 1939 (along with northern Bucovina) by the Soviet-German Non-Aggression Pact (the Molotov-Ribbentrop Pact) that also partitioned Poland. Many Romanians left the region at the time or were forced to leave; others were killed. The realignment of territories was recognised by the 1947 Paris Peace Treaty that formally ended the Second World War. This area of the former Soviet Socialist Republic of Moldavia is now the Republic of Moldova (and northern Bucovina, part of Ukraine).

On the Way to School *(page 65)*: In numerous Romanian fairy-tales, as characters flee giants or giantesses, monsters or spirits, the talismanic object of a brush or comb, or whetstone, needle, or ring (usually given to the heroes or heroines by a friendly guide or advisor), saves them; thrown back over the shoulder, these give rise to impediments like thick forests or stone mountains, create pure water, dispel evil fogs.

The Doctor *(page 67)*: The Danube–Black Sea Canal, started in May 1949, was an important part of the Romanian gulag of prisons and forced labour projects. It was built by slave labour – political prisoners, many of whom had no formal trial but who were thereafter marked for life as undesirable and unemployable. The canal was discontinued after Stalin's death on 5 March 1953; Ceauşescu later ordered that work be resumed, and the canal was completed.

The Brick Kiln *(page 74)*: The fox, geese, miller, hunters, etc. are from German children's songs. The other figures are from the legends that make up the Germanic epic poem of the Middle Ages known as the Nibelungenlied.

Emigration *(page 86)*: The Black Church in Braşov was built between 1383 and 1477; first it was Roman Catholic, then it became Lutheran during the Reformation. The Austrian army set fire to it in 1689. Having come under the Austrian protectorate in 1688, when Transylvania renounced Ottoman control, Braşov still resisted the Hapsburg forces a year later, and the burning of the church was in punishment for the city's disobedience. The fire blackened the church walls – hence its name. The Black Church is now famous for its organ and also for an extensive collection of Middle Eastern rugs, because of the practice of the region's Saxon tradesmen, who would donate their best rug to the church in thanksgiving after commercial trips to Turkey and the Middle East.

Ioana Ieronim, one of the most important and highly respected writers in contemporary Romania, is winning increasing international recognition. She is a prominent member of the generation of her country's writers who began their careers in the 1970s, a generation in which women were particularly notable both for their compelling artistry and for their engaged resistance to the repression and deprivation of Nicolae Ceauşescu's communist dictatorship. *The Triumph of the Water Witch* combines her devotion to poetry with a powerful evocation of the coming of communism to Romania and its effects on the sensitive spirit of the child who was the writer-to-be. Begun before the downfall of the Ceauşescu government, this is a book that its author expected never to see in print.

Ioana Ieronim was born in 1947 in the Transylvanian Saxon community of Râşnov in the Carpathian Mountains, the imaginative locale of the poems in this volume. She had a local German childhood education and then went on for further studies in Bucharest, graduating in 1970 from the University of Bucharest with a degree in English language and literature. Between 1979 and 1987 she published six books of poetry. Poems of hers from these collections, the majority in collaborative translations with Adam J. Sorkin but some others in renderings by Sorkin with Sergiu Celac, Romania's ambassador to Britain during the early 1990s, have appeared in numerous American and Canadian publications.

The Triumph of the Water Witch is Ieronim's seventh book and her first venture into prose poetry. It appeared in Romania in 1992, a little more than two years after the Romanian revolution. This English translation by Adam Sorkin and Ioana Ieronim was published by Bloodaxe Books in 2000.

Before the overthrow of the communist government in 1989, Ieronim worked for 15 years as an editor at the Scientific and Encyclopaedic Publishing House in Bucharest, where she lives. Since then, she has been on the editorial staff of cultural and political periodicals, served a four-year appointment as Cultural Counsellor in the Romanian Embassy in Washington, D.C., and coordinated public affairs for the Soros Foundation in Bucharest. At present, she is a Program Director for the Fulbright Commission in Romania.

Throughout her various activities during the recent decade of possibility in a newly freed Romania, Ieronim has continued to pursue her calling as a writer. Among her current literary projects, she is editing a selected volume of her poetry that will also gather recent poems not previously printed in book form.

Adam J. Sorkin has published twelve books of translations of contemporary Romanian poetry. *The Sky Behind the Forest* (Bloodaxe Books, 1997), a selection of Liliana Ursu's poems translated by him with Liliana Ursu and Tess Gallagher, was a Poetry Book Society Recommended Translation and was shortlisted for the Weidenfeld Prize. His translation of Marin Sorescu's final book, *The Bridge*, poems dictated from his sickbed, is due from Bloodaxe in 2001.

In 1999, Sorkin's translation of poems by Daniela Crăsnaru, *Sea-Level Zero*, mostly translated with the poet, was published by BOA Editions, and a small collection by Mircea Cărtărescu, *Bebop Baby*, done with various collaborators, came out in the Poetry New York Poetry Pamphlet Series. His 1998 anthology, *City of Dreams and Whispers*, a gathering of poets from the Moldavian cultural centre of Iași, won important honours in Romania.

Sorkin has been awarded support for his translation work from the Fulbright Scholar Program, the Rockefeller Foundation, the International Research & Exchanges Board (IREX), and the European Association for the Promotion of Poetry. In 1997 he won the International Quarterly Crossing Boundaries Translation Award, and in 1999 the Kenneth Rexroth Memorial Translation Prize. Sorkin is Professor of English at Penn State Delaware County, and a member of the American Literary Translators Association.